A THEORY OF HAPPINESS

(Fourth Edition)

QIGUANG LI, PH.D.

First published by China-Canada Institute of Happiness in February 2010

Second published in Shenzhen, China by China-Canada Institute of Happiness in April 2012

Library of Congress Catagoging-in-Publication Data
LI, Qiguang
    A theory of happiness/Qiguang LI.— 4th ed.
        p.   cm.
    Includes bibliographical references and index.
    ISBN 978-1530905652
    1. Happiness. 2. Subjective Well-Being.
    I. LI, Qiguang.   II. Title

Preface

What is happiness? For more than two millennia, since the time of the Greek philosophers, a definitive consensus for happiness has not been reached. There has been no powerful theory that can explain most of the data up to now (Diener, 2009a, pp.38-47).

There seems to be at least two reasons for this. One is that happiness is hard to measure. It can't be tested by empirical methods of science. The other is that there are many factors associated with happiness. In psychological questionnaires and neuroscientific experiments, it is difficult to change only one independent variable and keep the other independent variables unchanged. Thus, it is very difficult to establish a convincing causality of happiness.

An integrated theory of happiness (Wooden Bowl Model) is proposed in this book based on experimental results in neuroscience and evidence from surveys of happiness as well as evolutionism. This theory incorporates the major existing theories of happiness such as the "set-point" theory (Diener, 2009a, p.9) , the hedonic treadmill theory (Diener, 2009a, p.64), the comparison theory (Diener, 2009a, p.45), the adaptation theory (Diener, 2009a, p.45), the attention theory (Diener, 2009a, p.114), the goal theory(Diener, 2009a, p.38), the need theory (Diener, 2009a, p.38), the activity theory(Diener, 2009a, p.41), the judgment theory (Diener, 2009a, p.44), the top-down and bottom-up theories (Diener,

2009a, p.42), the evaluation theory (Diener, 2009a, p.139) and so forth.

In this integrated theory, biological factors and personality traits are attributed to hereditary factors that influence happiness. Factors such as culture, values are attributed to environmental factors that also influence happiness. Many concepts and methods borrowed from many fields such as physics, mathematics, economics, management, physiology, neuroscience, psychophysiology, psychophysics, sociology, philosophy as well as psychology are used to build the theory. For example, in order to find out and solve the primary problems, the approximation method in physics is used to simplify the complex components of happiness (i.e., positive affect, negative affect, and life satisfaction) (Diener, 2009a, p.70) into a single dimension. Secondary problems are considered by slight revisions and supplements.

Time is considered as a variable in the definition of happiness. The subjective emotional experiences are investigated in detail using seconds as the unit of time. As a result, it is possible to measure the amount of happiness with empirical methods.

While borrowing the concepts of intensity and duration from Bentham's definition of happiness (Bentham, 2006, p.29), this book does not fully agree with the stated utilitarian values. The dual nature of human selfishness and altruism is proposed based on the theory of "group selection" and the gene selfishness (Dawkins, 2006, p.7).

The detailed analyses are given in Chapter 7.

Like other social studies, the conclusions and inferences in the theory are drawn from statistical data. They are valid for the majority of people, but may not necessarily be applicable to every individual.

The theory is proposed in this book as a whole and each chapter is an indispensable part of the whole theory. Views or conclusions extracted from only part of the book may be incomplete or incorrect. Comments or criticisms from those who have patiently read the entire book are welcomed and appreciated.

In Chapter 1, the contradictions between the cognitive component of subjective well-being (SWB) and the empirical methods of science are analyzed (**subjective well-being is interchangeable with happiness in this book**). *Pleasure* and *happiness* linked to time are defined.

In Chapter 2, the *brain physiological state* is proposed which aims at:

(1) The *brain physiological state* can be measured by means of neuroscientific experiments.

(2) Multiple independent variables in experiments can be easily analyzed and manipulated.

(3) The relationships between the brain physiological quantity and psychological magnitude can be established.

In addition, all factors that influence the *brain physiological state* are analyzed by an illustrative figure. All external stimulation factors are classified into two categories. The factors included in the physical brain are analyzed.

Contributions of states of consciousness to the *brain physiological state* are classified. The *Equivalence Principle* is proposed. The major features of the *brain physiological state* are summarized in chapter 2.

In Chapter 3, sources and the physiological basis of *pleasure* are discussed. The time-dependency of *need* is analyzed. *Pleasure Intensity* is defined. The features of *Pleasure Intensity* are summarized based on the features of the *brain physiological state*. All emotional states are approximately grouped into three categories.

In Chapter 4, the *Preference of Attention* is proposed, and the features of *happiness* are given. Factors that influence *happiness* are classified into three categories. Necessary conditions for *happiness* are discussed.

In Chapter 5, *Need Intensity*, *Pleasure Intensity*, amount of *pleasure* in mathematics are defined. The purpose of these definitions is to help explain that: (1) *Need Intensity* and *Pleasure Intensity* can be assessed by psychological questionnaires. (2) The relationships between the brain physiological quantity and psychological magnitude can be established.

Methods of assessing the amount of *pleasure* are proposed. Experimental principles and methods for simultaneously measuring the brain physiological quantity and psychological magnitude are illustrated. Some specific experiments are designed. Hypothesized experimental results that can be tested in the future are predicted.

In Chapter 6, the amount of *happiness* in mathematics is defined. Scientific methods of measuring the amount of *happiness* are hypothesized. Happiness scales are discussed.

The *Weighted Scales* of *well-being* are presented. The index of *satisfaction level* at a moment in time and the index of *happiness level* during a period of time are defined.

In Chapter 7, the basic hypotheses and views of the theory are specified. A hierarchy of three stages for individuals' pursuits is proposed. Frequently asked questions are answered based on the features of *Pleasure Intensity* and *happiness*.

In Chapter 8, key elements and main conclusions of this theory are summarized. Elements from the major existing theories of happiness incorporated into this theory are listed. Contributions or possible contributions of this theory are summarized.

This book is academic. How individuals can actually be happier, and how governments or policymakers can build a happier society will be discussed in another book.

Email: happylife8@hotmail.com
Email: happylife99999@hotmail.com

Acknowledgments

This is the second English edition of my book, *A Theory of Happiness,* which was originally published in 2010. I am very grateful to Dr. Jiwei Wu, my former classmate, who proofread the entire book and provided valuable advices in English expressions. I am thankful to Michael Bossick, my English editor, who proofread most of the book. I would also like to thank my former classmates: Dr. Fucheng Wang, Dr. Yuhu Zhang, Dr. Weidong Tian, Dr. Yongqing Yang and others. Each of them proofread and provided English revisions to different parts of the book.

Contents

Chapter 1 Defining Happiness

Chapter 2 The Brain Physiological State

Chapter 3 Pleasure

Chapter 4 Happiness

Chapter 5 Measuring Pleasure

Chapter 6 Measuring Happiness

Chapter 7 Explanations of Certain Social Phenomena

Chapter 8 Summary and Conclusions

Chapter 1

Defining Happiness

Analyses of the Definition of Happiness

From antiquity to the present, "philosophers have debated the definition of happiness for millennia without reaching a definitive consensus. The concept of happiness differs, sometimes substantially, across theorists" (Diener, 2009a, p.176). There are numerous definitions of happiness. Only the widely used the definition of subjective well-being (SWB) is discussed in detail below. (**Subjective well-being is used synonymously with happiness in this book**).

1. Time-Dependency

"SWB refers to people's evaluations of their lives and encompasses both cognitive judgments of satisfaction and affective appraisals of moods and emotions" (Diener, 2009a, p.61). Andrews and Withey defined subjective well-being as "both cognitive evaluation and some degree of positive or negative feelings, i.e., affect" (Diener, 2009b, p.28). This definition does not contain the *time* factor. However, when people talk about happiness, there are two different situations linked to time. One is that people feel very happy during a shorter period of time such as seconds or minutes.

1

The other is that people live happy lives during a longer period of time such as the last several years or their whole past life.

2. Contradictions between the Cognitive Component of SWB and the Scientific Method

The cognitive evaluation is one component of subjective well-being. If researchers introduce *time* as a variable in the definition of subjective well-being, and analyze subjective well-being over time, they will find that the results of assessing subjective well-being at different times of evaluation are uncertain for the same event. This uncertainty leads to the non-unique results of cognitive evaluations of the same event. This means that the cognitive component in the definition of subjective well-being cannot be tested using scientific methods.

Diener gave at least two reasons for the non-uniqueness. First, "Differences in comparison standards are one reason that life satisfaction judgments may vary" (Diener, 2009b, p.48). "People may actually compare their lives to different standards in different circumstances" (Diener, 2009b, p.48). Second, "transient factors can influence life satisfaction judgments" (Diener, 2009b, p.49). "Schwarz and Clore showed that seemingly irrelevant factors such as the weather at the time of judgment can influence ratings of life satisfaction" (Diener, 2009b, p.76). "Current mood can influence ratings of life satisfaction, even if that current mood is not indicative of one's overall levels of affective well-being" (Diener, 2009b, p.76).

This book suggests that the considerable stability of long-term subjective well-being is not enough to build a scientific theory of subjective well-being, although "there are stabilities in life satisfaction across many years and across situations" (Diener, 2009b, p.49). From the scientific methodology, experimental results should be identical, unique and replicated no matter when and where the experiments are conducted under the same conditions. There is no any possibility that even one exceptional result appears.

The reason why theories of natural sciences such as physics and chemistry are convictive and widely accepted is due to the fact that the experimental results of the same event are unique and replicated under the same experimental conditions. The important reason why the scientific method has not been a powerful one in the understanding of subjective well-being so far is because the cognitive component of subjective well-being contradicts the empirical methods of science. Therefore, the results of the cognitive evaluation of life satisfaction can not be used as empirical evidence in the scientific study of happiness.

3. Response to the Challenge for the Hedonism Theory

The theory of happiness proposed in this book is different from the hedonic approach to happiness. Seligman et al. (2003) wrote, "one basic challenge facing a hedonist is that when we wish someone a happy life (or a happy childhood, or even a happy week), we are not merely wishing that they accumulate a tidy sum of pleasures, irrespective of how this sum is distributed across one's life-span or its meaning for the whole. We can imagine two lives that contain the same exact amount of momentary pleasantness, but one life tells a story of gradual decline (ecstatic childhood, light-hearted youth, dysphonic adulthood, miserable old age) while another is a tale of gradual improvement (the above pattern in reverse). The difference between these lives is a matter of their global trajectories and these cannot be discerned from the standpoint of its individual moments". The view taken by this proposed theory is that the two lives contain totally different amount of momentary pleasantness because of the features of *Pleasure Intensity* such as *Integration, Relativity, Equivalence,* as well as the *Preference of Attention* which will be described later in this book. While thinking of better life in the future, an individual easily feels pleasant. While thinking of worse life in the future, an individual easily feels unpleasant. Therefore, in the life of gradual improvement, an individual experienced more positive feelings when the individual made cognitive evaluation of future, whereas in the life of gradual decline, an individual experienced more negative feelings when the individual made cognitive evaluation of future.

4. Simplification and Approximation

In physics, approximation methods are often used to analyze problems. Complex problems can be first simplified using approximation methods, i.e. the primary problems are found out and solved first, secondary problems are considered by slight revisions and supplements. For example, the Energy Band Theory (Grosso, 2006) came from the simplified methods used to get the complex differential equations solved in solid state physics. As a result, mobile phones, computers and the internet have all been widely applied.

The bottom-up theory suggests that happiness is the sum of many small pleasures or the sum of momentary pleasures and pains (Diener, 2009a, p.42). "Affect Balance Scale (ABS) score is derived by subtracting the sum of negative items from the sum of positive ones" (Diener, 2009a, p.18). The definition of happiness from the bottom-up theory is closer to the laws of empirical science. Therefore, the multiple components of subjective well-being could be first simplified into a single dimension in order to find and solve the primary problems. Secondary problems can be considered by slight revisions and supplements afterwards. "Most researchers agree with Cannon and Bard that our experienced emotions also involve cognition" (Myers, 2004, p.501). A cognitive evaluation always occurs during a short period of time. The result of evaluation can be approximately thought of as the subjective emotional experience at the time of evaluation. The cognitive component of subjective well-being can be approximately attributed to the affective component of subjective well-being when measuring happiness during a longer period of time.

The Definitions of Pleasure and Happiness

How do people spend their lives? People spend their entire lives day by day, minute by minute, second by second. If a person experiences more pleasant than unpleasant events in one day, then he or she has a happy day. If a person experiences frequent positive affect and rare negative affect in his or her lifetime, he or she has a happy life.

The pleasure or happiness in this book refers to subjective feelings, or subjective emotional experiences. Whether a person is happy or not is his or her own subjective experience, regardless of how others see it (Diener, 2009a, p.1).

This book stresses the time-dependency of happiness. Subjective emotional experience changes over time.

The italicized term **pleasure** is defined as the sum of all positive feelings or positive emotions (Diener, 2009b, p.140) or positive affects in this book. *Pleasure* is approximated as a single dimension, regardless of arousal and multiple components. *Pleasure* stands for positive emotional states described by words such as delighted, comfortable, pleasant, pleased, glad, excited, happy, elated, content, proud, cheerful, optimistic, enjoyment, interested, funny, amused, merry, joyful, rapturous, satisfied, ecstasy, gratification, in a good mood, and so forth. *Pleasure* includes "the pleasures of the intellect, of the feelings and imagination, and of the moral sentiments" (Mill, 2003, p.187). *Pleasure* includes mental and bodily pleasures, real and illusive pleasures. *Pleasure* stands for positive emotional experiences during a shorter period of time. A shorter period of time can be seconds, tens of seconds, tens of minutes, or hours. In other words, *pleasure* is linked to a shorter period of time.

The term **pain** is defined as the sum of all negative feelings or negative emotions or negative affects in this book. *Pain* is approximated as a single dimension. *Pain* stands for negative emotional states described by words such as suffering, misfortune, painful, distressed, grief, miserable, discomfort, uncomfortable, fear, anxious, anger, depression, sad, nervous, jealous, envious, irritable, gloomy, lonely, solemn, tortured, unhappy, disappointed, angry, embarrassed, annoyed, disgusted, shamed, nausea, rage, sorrow, failure, in a bad mood, and so forth. *Pain* includes mental and bodily pains, real and illusive pains. *Pain* is the semantic antonym of *pleasure*. *Pain* stands for negative emotional experiences during a shorter period of time. In other words, *pain* is linked to a shorter period of time.

The italicized term **happiness** is defined as the sum of *pleasures* minus the sum of *pains*, or the sum of many small *pleasures* (*pain* can be thought of as the negative of *pleasure*) during a longer period of time. A longer period of time can be years, decades or a lifetime. *Pleasure* during a shorter period of time is a fraction of *happiness* during a longer period of time. *Happiness* is the aggregation of *pleasures* across time, an accumulation of happy moments. *Happiness* is linked to a longer period of time.

For example, during four years at college, if a person experienced far more pleasant than unpleasant events and had much more pleasant time than unpleasant time, it could be said that the person was quite happy in his or her college days.

If a person experienced many pleasant events, very rare

unpleasant events, and had much more pleasant time than unpleasant time in his or her lifetime, the person would be considered to have a very happy life.

Basic Hypotheses

This theory also has the following three basic hypotheses.

(1) Human has the dual nature of selfishness and altruism.

(2) Individuals' survival and reproduction are primary, and individuals' pursuits of *pleasure* and *happiness* are secondary.

(3) Rational individuals pursue long-term *happiness*, rather than short-term *pleasure*.

The theory of evolution is the foundation of above hypotheses. More detailed explanations will be given in Chapter 7 with examples.

Chapter 2

The Brain Physiological State

The Basis of Pleasure and Happiness

The brain is the physical basis of *pleasure* and *happiness*. According to cognitive neuroscience, "everything psychological is simultaneously neurological" (Solso, 2005, p.35). "All cognition is the result of neurological activity" (Solso, 2005, p.36). *Pleasure* and *happiness* are the result of neurological activity in the brain which is the platform where an individual experiences *pleasure* and *happiness.*

Take eating as an example, "it is equipped with about three thousand taste buds, tiny little nubs a few hundredths of a millimeter high, mainly on the tongue. Each of these little bumps contains about fifty sense cells that respond to the different tastes". "Altogether, more than a hundred thousand nerve strands, bundled into two cords, pass taste information from the tongue to the brain. In addition, there are sensors that report heat and cold, and others that identify texture—whether it's soft or crunchy, moist or dry. Cotton candy tastes different from caramel, although both are made of sugar. Finally, there are those sensors that register burning and thus respond to the spiciness of chilies. Every bite and every movement of the tongue sets off an entire firework display of electric signals" (Klein, 2006, p.110). The electric signals are quickly passed to the brain.

The Brain Physiological State

The physiological state of the brain is always changing even while sleeping. "The brain is always alive with electrochemical activity, and an excited neuron may fire as often as one thousand times per second". "These firings can be observed by means of electroencephalograph (EEG) and event-related potential (ERP) recordings, which measure the electrical activities of regions of the brain" (Solso, 2005, p.41).

As the brain is the platform of feeling and experiencing *pleasure*, the term **brain physiological state** is defined in this book to describe the overall physiological states of the brain at any moment in time. The purpose of this definition is to construct a bridge between the physiological quantity and the psychological magnitude of the brain at the same moment in time. The physiological quantity can be measured by means of scientific experiments, in the meantime, the psychological magnitude can be obtained by questionnaires.

The *brain physiological state $B(t)$* is defined as follows:

$B = B(t)$ is a function of time t. $B(t)$ is a physiological quantity which is a combination of physiological states of the brain at the time t.

$B(t)$ contains all of the electrical parameters, chemical parameters, and physiological parameters of the brain.

B(t) is a set of all parameters.

$B(t) = \{B_1, B_2, ... B_i, ... B_n\}$, where B_1, B_2, ... B_i, ... B_n are elements of *B*. These elements of the set $\{B_1, B_2, ... B_i, ... B_n\}$ describe the *brain physiological state* at the time *t*.

Any element B_i of *B* can be measured by means of scientific experiments. Each element describes one aspect of the *brain physiological state*. All elements together describe the *brain physiological state* as a whole.

For example, in electroencephalogram (EEG) (Luck, 2005, p.3), *B(t)* contains brain waves such as alpha, theta, delta waves and so forth (Solso, 2005, p.152). In event-related potential (ERP), *B(t)* contains ERP components such as C1, N1, N2, N400, P1, P2, P3, MMN (mismatch negativity) and LRP (lateralized readiness potential) (Luck, 2005, pp.35-49).

B(t) contains all images of cerebral activity recorded by a Mental Activity Network Scanner (MANSCAN)(Solso, 2005, p.52).

B(t) contains blood flow and other information from experiments in functional Magnetic Resonance Imaging (fMRI)(Solso, 2005, p.56).

B(t) also includes the level of blood glucose, amount of dopamine, oxytocin, beta-endorphon, acetylcholine, cortisol, bata-endorphin, endorphin, enkephalin, dynorphin, morphine, heroin, vasopressin, corticotrophin-releasing hormone, serotonin (Klein, 2006, pp.34-167) and other substances in the brain.

B(t) contains the brain blood pressure, temperature and other vital signs at the time *t*.

All of the measurable parameters in experiments are

elements of *B(t)*.

The term **baseline state** or **ground state** $B_0(t)$ of *B(t)* is defined as Stage IV sleep (Luck, 2005, p.236; Foot, 2009, p.45; Solso, 2005, p.153).

"In Stage IV sleep, the EEG recordings are similar to those of the precious stage, but more extensive delta waves are noted. Stage IV sleep is the deepest of sleep states, from which arousal is most difficult" (Solso, 2005, p.153).

In other words, there is no *pleasure,* no consciousness in the *ground state $B_0(t)$*.

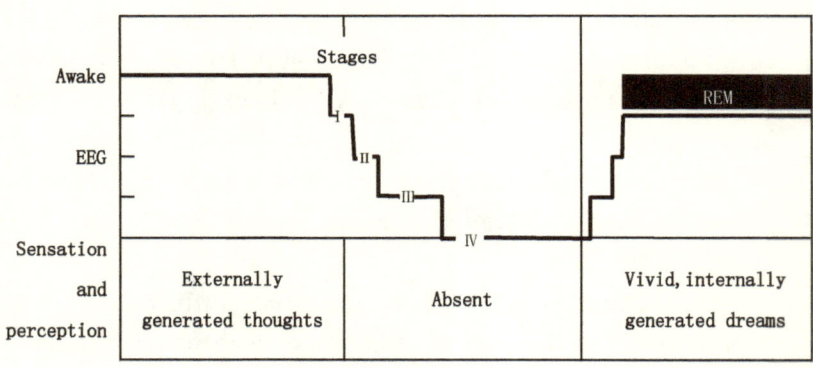

Figure 2.1 Sleep Cycle (Solso, 2005, p.153)

In Stage IV sleep, the parameters of EEG constitute some elements of $B_0(t)$. Additional physiological parameters measured using the other techniques constitute the other elements of $B_0(t)$.

The features of the *ground state $B_0(t)$* are summarized as follows:

(1) Each individual's $B_0(t)$ is different. $B_0(t)$ contains all

individuals' hereditary factors such as blood type, skin color, personality traits, etc. $B_0(t)$ is also related to environmental factors such as values, culture, religion and so forth. $B_0(t)$ describes the state of the physical brain with unconsciousness.

(2) The *ground state* $B_0(t)$ changes over time, but generally changes very slowly. Like an individual's appearance, it is changing every day, but the changes can not be easily identified in the short term. Environmental factors leave their traces in the brain every day. "Furthermore, unlike rats, humans are not shaped by their childhood once and for all, something Davidson discovered when he asked those people whose brainwaves he'd measured when they were babies to return to his lab ten years later. Now they were school children, and the patterns of their brainwaves showed little relation to those of the decade before" (Klein, 2006, p.47).

Researchers can track and record an individual's EEG of Stage IV sleep by means of long-term experiments, and observe the changes in $B_0(t)$ over time.

(3) The *ground state* $B_0(t)$ can be used as the absolute baseline of amplitude in quantitative measurements of ERP (Luck, 2005, p.236).

The *ground state* $B_0(t)$ can approximately correspond to a happiness *set-point* (Carr, 2005, p.21). A happiness *set-point* can then be measured with scientific methods such as EEG.

Factors Influencing the Brain Physiological State

The *brain physiological state* describes the overall physiological states of the brain at any time. Figure 2.2 illustrates all the factors that influence the *brain physiological state B(t)*. The *brain physiological state B(t)* at the time *t* is the integrated result of the interaction of all external stimuli and internal physiological factors, as well as the state of consciousness at the time *t*.

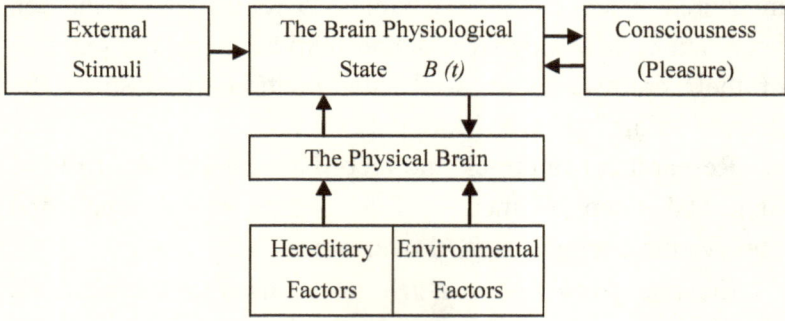

Figure 2.2 Factors Influencing the *Brain Physiological State*

External Factors

There are many external stimuli to the *brain physiological state B(t)*. In order to facilitate the analysis of issues, all external stimuli are classified into two categories.

(1) *External physical stimulation*

"The sensory system is composed of the receptors and connecting neurons of the five senses (hearing, sight, touch, taste, and smell)" (Solso, 2005, p.75).

External physical stimulation is passed to the brain through the sensory system, and causes changes in the *brain physiological state B(t).*

Table 2.1   The Five Senses (Solso, 2005, p.73)

Sense	Structure	Stimulus	Receptor
Vision	Eye	Light waves	Rods and cones
Hearing	Ear	Sound waves	Hair cells
Taste	Tongue	Chemicals	Taste buds
Smell	Nose	Chemicals	Hair cells
Touch	Skin	Pressure	Nerve cells

(2) *External Informational Stimulation*

External informational stimulation is passed to the brain through physical quantities perceived by the sensory system, and causes changes in the *brain physiological state B(t)*. For example, when the brain receives the information such as winning a big prize, being admitted to a famous university, or getting a good job offer, changes in electrochemical activity take place in the brain and simultaneously the *brain physiological state B(t)* changes.

The above classification is only a method of classification. Physical stimulation and informational stimulation often exist simultaneously. Informational stimulation is based on physical stimulation.

The difference between informational and physical stimulation lies in different emphases. Informational stimulation emphasizes the effect of information itself, not physical quantity, on the brain. In this case, the physical quantity is just the carrier of information. When a person knows that he or she has won a big prize, what he or she perceives does not sound good or look good, but the brain receives the information the sound or the words convey. The external information doesn't make the sensory system feel good or bad, but influences individuals' consciousness. An individual's subjective experience is the same whether the person hears or reads the news. Physical stimulation emphasizes the effect of physical quantity on the brain. The music sounds good, the picture looks good, the physical stimulation does not emphasize the information such as feelings or thoughts contained in either the music or the picture. *External physical stimulation* focuses on effects on an individual's sensory system.

Physical stimulation and informational stimulation often appear in a process simultaneously. A good symphony has a beautiful melody as well as a moving emotional expression. In the process of hearing the symphony, the brain receives both physical stimulation and informational stimulation simultaneously.

External stimuli can be classified according to time. Some external stimuli are short-term, such as watching a football game, while others are cyclical such as eating and drinking. Some stimuli are transient such as lightning, while others can be long-term, such as stress from work and some are continuous such as being lovelorn.

External stimuli can be classified according to the consequences of stimulation, some stimulating effects will disappear quickly and others take a longer time to fade away. Factors influencing consequences of stimulation are: stimulus intensity, stimulus complexity, the importance of the stimulus and the repetition interval of stimuli.

Generally, the stronger the intensity of the stimulus, the more complex and important the stimulus, the longer the duration the stimulus interval, then the longer the effects of the stimulus continue.

The Physical Brain

There are two kinds of internal factors influencing the *brain physiological state B(t)*. One is the physical brain. The human brain consists of the physical brain and states of consciousness (or Body and Mind) (Solso, 2005, p.35). The physical brain refers to material brain, bodily brain, the state of the brain without consciousness or the brain at the *ground state $B_0(t)$*."The human brain is densely packed with neurons. Some estimates place the number at more than 100 billion" (Solso, 2005, p.38). "In addition to blood and water, more than sixty different transmitters circulate within it—molecules that have an enormous effect on our actions and feelings" (Klein, 2006, p.80).

1. The physical brain includes hereditary factors and environmental factors

"A normal human, then, is a product of both hereditary and environmental factors" (Hughes, 2002, p.68). "Nature and nurture together form who we are. As the area of a field is determined by both its length and width, so do biology and experience together create us" (Myers, 2005, p.9).

In the process of an individual's growth, environmental factors leave memory traces in the brain. "Behavior influences the functions of the brain, and that influences the brain's architecture, so that experience produces lasting effects in the structure and function of the brain" (Hughes, 2002, p.70).

(1) Hereditary factors

At the time of birth, the physical brain is determined only by hereditary factors. Hereditary factors include individuals' genes, blood type, skin color and other individuals' characteristics. Hereditary factors include individuals' respiratory, digestive, circulatory, reproductive, nervous, locomotive, endocrine and urinary systems, plus other physiological factors. Hereditary factors also include personality traits and so forth.

(2) Environmental factors

Environmental factors for an individual include times, climate, region, social system, culture, ethics, and law as well as the individual's living environment, education, experiences, habits, values, religious belief and so forth.

2. The physical brain is constantly changing

At any moment, the state of the physical brain is

influenced by a person's physiological systems: respiratory, digestive, circulatory, reproductive, nervous, locomotive, urinary system, etc. The state of any organ influences the state of the physical brain. All information from physiological changes in all organs can be passed to the brain instantly. For example, the information about a stomachache being passed to the brain through the nervous system causes changes in the *brain physiological state B(t)*, and causes the person to subjectively feel the stomachache at the same time.

The overall physiological states of the body are constantly changing over time. Since the metabolic system is functioning in the body continually, the physical brain is changing all the time. The brain today is different from the brain yesterday. Although the short-term differences are small, in the long-term, changes in the brain are huge. There is a big difference between the brain of 30-year-old and the brain of 20-year-old. "The brain can change as the individual grows into adulthood" (Klein, 2006, p.47).

An imperfect analogy follows to illustrate the physical brain (Wooden Bowl Model).

The physical brain is like a rice bowl made of wood – a *wooden bowl*. Using the bowl to have meals can cause a small amount of food to penetrate into the wood material. Like different individuals having different hereditary factors, *wooden bowls* are made of different wood materials. Just as environmental factors can leave different memory traces in the brain between different individuals, the ingredients and amount of foods penetrated into the *wooden bowl* differ between different *wooden bowls*. A 20-year-old *wooden bowl* is different from a 30-year-old *wooden bowl* because a 30-year-old *wooden bowl* has ten more years experience holding the food.

If subjective emotional experience is compared to the sensual taste of foods, each time when eating, the taste of foods includes the smell of current foods, the smell of the wood material and the smell of the foods the bowl held before. In other words, at any moment in time, the taste of foods (subjective emotional experiences) in the *wooden bowl* is related to the wood material (hereditary factors) that the bowl was made of, the smell of the foods the bowl currently contains (external stimuli for the time being), and the smell of foods the bowl held previously (environmental factors), plus the brain state of consciousness at the moment.

States of Consciousness

Another internal factor influencing the *brain physiological state* is states of consciousness, or conscious activity at a waking state.

"Consciousness is the awareness of environmental and cognitive events such as the sights and sounds of the world as well as of one's memories, thoughts, feelings, and bodily sensations" (Solso, 2005, p.141). States of consciousness refer to the states of conscious activity, "for example, thinking, holding things in memory, perceiving, judging, as well as being in love, feeling pain, plotting schemes to rule the world, composing music, and making jokes" (Solso,

2005, p. 36).

The *brain physiological states* differ between consciousness and unconsciousness."The clearest distinction between consciousness and unconscious is seen when one is awake or sleep" (Solso, 2005, p.151). "When full consciousness returns from deep sleep, a massive change in electrical activity takes place all over the brain, as the fast, small, and irregular waves of waking EEG replace the large, slow, and regular hills and valleys of deep sleep" (Solso, 2005, p.141).

A person has no consciousness in deep sleep, under global anesthesia, in a coma or in a vegetative state. The *brain physiological states* are different in different states of consciousness. "The physical changes in neural activity cause changes in the mind" (Solso, 2005, p.36). The *brain physiological state B(t)* at the time *t* determines the states of consciousness at the time *t*. Simultaneously, states of consciousness also influence the *brain physiological state B(t)*. There is a bidirectional influence between states of consciousness and the *brain physiological state B(t)* (Larsen, 2008, p.185). The mutual influence and interaction between states of consciousness and the *brain physiological state* reach a dynamic equilibrium.

"Consciousness occurs in varied states" (Myers, 2004, p.268). In order to facilitate the analysis of issues, states of consciousness are classified into the following categories.

1. *State of Need*

The *State of Need* refers to the state when a person subjectively desires to get something or to have some needs met. There are desires such as eating, drinking or having sex. For example, when a person is hungry, the person has a desire to get something to eat. In the *State of Need*, a person has at least one *need*.

The *State of Need* contributes to *B(t)*.

2. *State of Pleasure*

The *State of Pleasure* refers to the state when a person experiences positive feelings or positive emotions, also includes negative feelings or emotions—*pain* that can be thought of as the negative of *pleasure*.

The subjective emotional state contributes to *B(t)*.

3. *State of Thinking*

"Thinking is a process by which a new mental representation is formed through the transformation of information by complex interaction of the mental attributes of judging, abstracting, reasoning, imagining, and problem solving" (Solso, 2005, p.418). "Thought, or thinking, refers to the general process of considering an issue in the mind" (Solso, 2005, p.422). For example, merely by closing his or her eyes and lying down, a person thinks of something without any activity and changes in external stimulation.

The *State of Thinking* defined here includes judging, abstracting, reasoning, imagining, associating, decision making, and so forth. It excludes the *State of Remembering the Past* and the *State of Imagining the Future* defined below.

The *State of Thinking* contributes to *B(t)*.

4. *State of Remembering the Past*

The *State of Remembering the Past* refers to the state of emotional experience when the brain remembers the past events.

An event that happened in the past contributes to the current $B(t)$.

5. *State of Imagining the Future*

The *State of Imagining the Future* refers to the state of emotional experience when the brain imagines or expects future events.

A future event that does not happen at the present time contributes to the current $B(t)$.

6. *State of Cognition*

"The term 'cognition' refers to all processes by which the sensory input is transformed, reduced, elaborated, stored, recovered, and used ... it is apparent that cognition is involved in everything a human being might possibly do" (Solso, 2005, p.2). The *State of Cognition* refers to the state when a person makes a cognitive evaluation.

Because the *brain physiological state* changes in the cognitive process, the *State of Cognition* contributes to $B(t)$.

7. *State of Meditation*

Meditation focuses attention on the present moment or a fixed stimulus such as one's breath or a mantra (Carr, 2005, p.219). "The person meditating always directs his perception towards a simple focus" (Klain, 2006, p.226).

The *State of Meditation* contributes to $B(t)$.

8. Other States

Other States refer to the states that are not included in the states mentioned above.

There are no strict boundaries in the above classifications. One state of consciousness and the other states of consciousness often exist at the same time. For example, the *State of Remembering the Past* and the *State of Pleasure* can exist simultaneously, and so can the *State of Cognition* and the *State of Pleasure*. The *State of Cognition* may contain the *State of Thinking*, the *State of Remembering the Past,* or the *State of Imagining the Future* and so forth at the same time.

The above classification is intended to describe:

The *State of Need* at the time t influences $B(t)$. The *State of Pleasure* at the time t influences $B(t)$. The *State of Thinking* at the time t influences $B(t)$. The *State of Cognition* at the time t influences $B(t)$. The *State of Meditation* at the time t influences $B(t)$. Events that happened prior to the time t can influence the current $B(t)$ when the brain remembers these events. Future events that do not happen at the time t can influence the current $B(t)$ when the brain thinks of these events that may happen, must happen or can not happen in the future.

States of consciousness in the brain are constantly changing along with the changes in time and the surrounding environment. Sometimes the *State of Need* is predominant and sometimes the *State of Cognition* is predominant. Sometimes, states of consciousness are in the *State of Thinking*, while other times they are in the *State of*

Remembering the Past or in the *State of Imagining the Future*. Sometimes, states of consciousness are in the state of *pleasure* or *pain.*

What attention is focused on at any time determines the predominant state of consciousness at the time.

The Equivalence Principle

In physics, the concept of equivalence is often used to analyze problems. Complex problems may be significantly simplified by using the equivalence principle. Examples include the equivalence principle in the theory of relativity (Cheng, 2005, p.38), the equivalent circuit in an electric circuit (Richard, 2001, p.167), and so forth.

The ***Equivalence Principle*** borrowed from physics is defined in this book as an event that will not happen in the future, but may influence the *brain physiological state $B(t)$* if an individual subjectively believes that this event will definitely happen. This kind of influence is the same as the influence when the event actually happens in the future. Equivalence means that two different external events have identical objective impacts on the *brain physiological state $B(t)$*.

Imagine a scenario that helps explain the *Equivalence Principle* below.

A man's current monthly salary is $5,000. He is looking for a higher paying job. He is excited when he receives a new job offer (an external stimulus) from a company because the new job pays $10,000 a month in a better work environment, is closer to home, has less responsibility and more room for future career development. In short, the new job is much better than the current one. But it will not start for two weeks. He feels quite pleasant when he thinks about this new job, or when he talks about the job with his friends, relatives and family members during the week after he gets the good news.

Two situations are analyzed below.

(1) The new job does not start immediately, but will start in two weeks. This indicates that the event that will definitely happen in the future and it has an impact on the current *brain physiological state B(t)*. As a result, he feels elated.

(2) Let's assume that, a week later, he is informed from the company that the new job offer is withdrawn owing to an accident. He will not get the new job. His feeling of *pleasure* immediately evaporates at the time when he is notified about the withdrawal of the job offer.

However, during the week from getting the new job offer to the subsequent withdrawal of it, the new job prospect makes him pleasant. This indicates that the event (getting the new job) which will not happen in the future also has an impact on the current *brain physiological state B(t)* as long as he subjectively believes that the new job information is true and reliable.

A comparison of situations (1) and (2) shows that the *brain physiological state B(t)* is not related to whether the new job exists or not during the week from getting the new job offer to the subsequent withdrawal of it. In other words, after two weeks, his starting the new job (a future event) and his not starting the new job (another future event)—these two different external events have identical impacts on his brain during the week from getting the new job offer to the subsequent withdrawal of it.

This is because the human brain cannot distinguish the difference between one event that will happen in the future, and another event that is subjectively believed to happen definitely in the future, even if this event is an impossible occurrence.

An important inference is that a future event that does not happen at the present time may influence an individual's current emotional experiences and cognitive evaluations.

Features of the Brain Physiological State

Figure 2.3 illustrates the features of the *brain physiological state B(t)*.

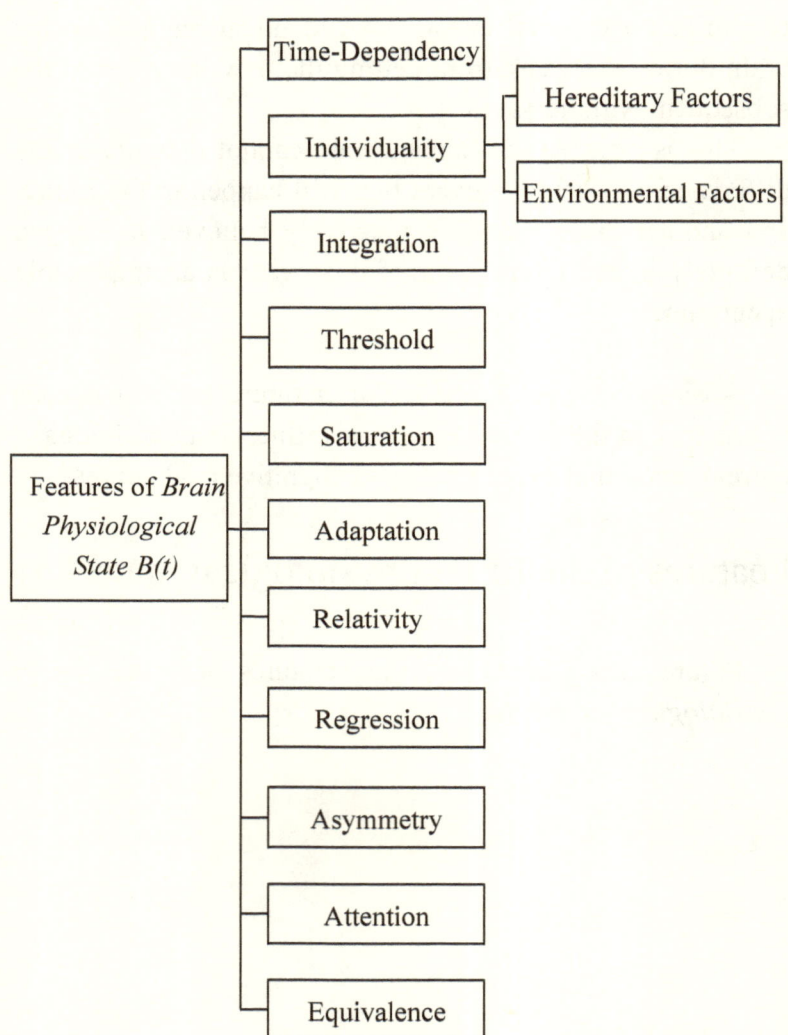

Figure 2.3 Features of the *Brain Physiological State*

1. *Time-Dependency*
   The *brain physiological state B(t)* is constantly changing

over time. As long as a person is alive, the changes in his or her *brain physiological state B(t)* over time will never stop.

2. *Individuality*

Each individual's brain is different because the hereditary factors and environmental factors of each individual are different. In the growth process, each individual's natural environment and social environment are also different.

3. *Integration*

"Happiness and unhappiness have their own brain circuits and their own chemistry. But this doesn't mean that pleasant and unpleasant emotions are independent of one another. Though we can be both sad and cheerful, normally we're one or the other. The brain systems for negative and positive feelings are entwined in such a way that a good feeling can prevent bad ones and vice versa" (Klein, 2006, p.37). "Most of the processes in the brain are determined by the interplay of two opposing players, and the emotional circuits function the same way. Positive feelings can extinguish negative ones, and vice versa" (Klein, 2006, p.38).

The *brain physiological state B(t)* is the integrated result of the interaction of all external stimuli and internal physiological factors, as well as the state of consciousness at the time *t*. This integrated result does not have the characteristics of the superposition principle in physics. This result is neither the linear superposition, nor the non-linear superposition. The integrated result related to the states of consciousness does not follow an unchanging law.

The degree of contribution from a stimulus to the *brain*

physiological state B(t) is determined not only by the stimulus intensity and duration, but also by the attention at the time *t*.

External stimulation influences the *brain physiological state B(t)*. Responses of the *brain physiological state B(t)* to external stimulation have the features of *Threshold, Saturation, Adaptation, Relativity, Regression, Asymmetry* and *Equivalence*. These features are discussed respectively below.

4. *Threshold*

Threshold refers to only when the intensity of an external stimulus exceeds a certain magnitude — a threshold, can this stimulus influence *B(t)*, and cause a response in the brain to the stimulus.

There is a threshold for each external stimulus. Thresholds are different for different external stimuli. Stimulation thresholds for different individuals are different, depending on hereditary factors. For an identical external stimulus, there are response differences between individuals.

For some external factors, the thresholds are time-dependent. The thresholds of these factors changes along with the changes in time and the surrounding environment. For example, the food thresholds differ between hunger and being satiated. The sex thresholds differ before and after sexual intercourse.

The physiological basis of *Threshold* is:

"The sensory information must be of a certain magnitude to be perceived" (Solso, 2005, p.7). For example, as Table 2.2 shows, only when the concentration of sodium chloride exceeds 2000 (μmol / L), can people perceive a salty taste.

Table 2.2 Some Taste Thresholds (Ganong, 1995, p.172)

Substance	Taste	Threshold concentration (μmol/L)
Hydrochloric acid	Sour	100
Sodium chloride	Salt	2000
Strychnine hydrochloride	Bitter	1.6
Glucose	Sweet	80,000
Sucrose	Sweet	10,000
Saccharin	Sweet	23

5. *Saturation*

Saturation (Alexander, 2000, p.168) or ceiling effects (Diener, 2009b, p. 17) means that increasingly stronger external stimuli cause increasingly larger responses in the brain, until the point of maximum response is reached. At this point (saturation level), increasing the intensity does not produce any more responses, the *brain physiological state B(t)* reaches the state of *saturation* that is the brain physiological limit to the stimuli.

There is a saturation level for each external stimulus. Saturation levels differ for different external stimuli. Saturation levels for different individuals are also different, depending on hereditary factors. Saturation levels for an identical external stimulus differ between individuals.

For some external stimuli, the saturation levels are time-dependent. The saturation levels for these stimuli change along with the changes in time and the surrounding environment.

The physiological basis of *Saturation* is:

Physiological responses of human organs are limited, according to physiological psychology. For example, "Increasingly stronger doses of a drug cause increasingly larger effects, until the point of maximum effect is reached. At this point, increasing the dose of the drug does not produce any more effect" (Carlson, 2005, p.98).

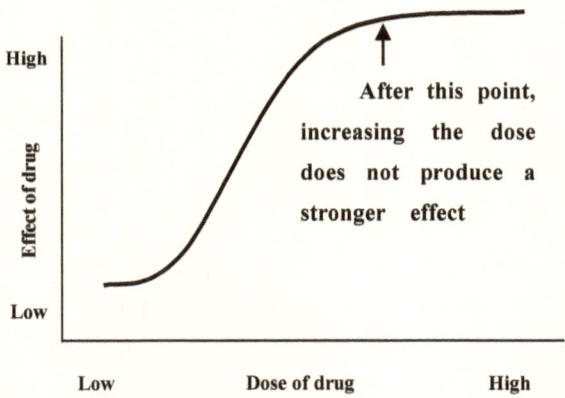

Figure 2.4 A dose-response curve. Increasingly stronger doses of a drug produce increasingly larger effects until the maximum effect is reached. After that point, increments in the dose do not produce any increments in the drug's effect (Carlson, 2005, p.98).

6. *Adaptation*

There are two implications for *Adaptation* of the brain to external stimulation.

(1) *Diminishing Marginal Response*

In economics, "additional increments of the same good or service, within some stated period of time, will yield smaller and smaller increments of pleasure. These increments of pleasure are called marginal utility, and the general tendency of marginal utility to diminish is called the law of *diminishing marginal utility*" (Heilbroner, 1987, p.137).

Similarly, additional increments of the external stimulus intensity, within some stated period of time, will yield smaller and smaller increments of response in the brain.

The physiological basis of *diminishing marginal response* is:

In psychophysics, *Fechner's law* states that the strength of a sensation grows as the logarithm of stimulus intensity,

$$S=k\log I$$

where S stands for psychological (that is, subjective) magnitude, I for stimulus intensity, and k is a constant (Gleitman, 1987, p.116).

"The range of stimulus intensities to which we are sensitive is enormous. We can hear sounds as weak as the ticking of a watch twenty feet away and as loud as a pneumatic drill operating right next to us. Our nervous system has to have a mechanism to compress this huge range into some manageable scope, and this is precisely what a logarithmic transformation does for us" (Gleitman, 1987, p.116).

This implies that the response in the brain to external stimulation is **diminishing marginal response.**

(2) *Adaptation*

"Investigators have known for a long time that a moderate, constant stimulus applied to the skin fails to produce any sensation after it has been present for a while". "Physiological studies have shown that the reason for the lack of the sensation is the absence of receptor firing; the receptors adapt to a constant stimulus" (Carlson, 2005, p.209). "After constant exposure to a stimulus, our nerve cells fire less frequently" (Myers, 2004, p.198). "These examples illustrate sensory adaptation-our diminishing sensitivity to an unchanging stimulus" (Myers, 2004, p.198).

The physiological basis of *Adaptation* is:

"This adaptation is not caused by 'fatigue' of physical or chemical processes within the receptor. Instead, adaptation occurs because of the physical construction of the skin and the cutaneous sensory organs" (Carlson, 2005, p.209).

This implies that *Adaptation* derived from human sensory organs is intrinsic.

The essence of *Adaptation* is beneficial to survival, and is beneficial for an organism to adapt to environments. *Adaptation* is a consequence of evolution of organism.

7. *Relativity*

Relativity means that the magnitude of response in the brain to the latter external stimulus is dependent on the consequences of the previous stimulus. For example, one perceives a sweet taste when eating pastries after drinking water. However, one doesn't taste and feel sweet when eating pastries after eating a piece of candy.

"Feelings of warmth and coolness are relative, not absolute (except at the extremes). There is a temperature level that, for a particular region of skin, will produce a sensation of temperature neutrality—neither warmth nor coolness. This neutral point is not an absolute value but depends on the prior history of thermal stimulation of the area" (Carlson, 2005, p.209).

This relativity in the feeling to ambient temperature can be demonstrated easily by placing one hand in a bucket of warm water and the other in a bucket of cool water until some adaptation has taken place. If you then simultaneously immerse both hands in water at room temperature, it will feel warm to one hand and cool to the other (Carlson, 2005, pp.209-210).

The physiological basis of *Relativity* is:

In psychophysiology, the **law of initial value** (LIV) "says that the magnitude of phasic change in a response system is dependent on the tonic prestimulus base level". "In general terms, the higher the prestimulus level, the smaller is the potential response increase, and the larger is the potential response decrease under equal stimulus conditions" (Hugdahl, 1995, pp.38-39).

8. *Regression*

Regression means that when an external stimulus is canceled, the brain activation gradually returns to its original state without the external stimulus. Suppose a person is having an interview for a big job. Because of nervousness, his or her heart rate speeds up. However, the heart rate will return to normal afterwards.

"Regression toward the mean" refers to the tendency for unusual events to "regress" toward their average state. Thus, extraordinary happenings tend to be followed by more ordinary ones (Myers, 2004, p.676).

The physiological basis of *Regression* is:

When activated areas in the brain are not inputted with a stimulus signal, the brain activation levels diminish over time (TANG, 2000, p.15).

"We can't endure this pleasant laziness for too long, for the effect of opioids lasts only a short while—between a few minutes and a few hours, depending on the situation" (Klein, 2006, p.117). "If the efficacy of the happiness drug wanes, our 'normal' mood returns, and after the prior euphoria this can be perceived as an intolerable decline" (Klein, 2006, p.117).

The difference between *Regression* and *Adaptation* is that *Regression* describes the brain activity after external stimulation within a shorter period of time is canceled, while *Adaptation* describes the response in the brain to external stimulation that is sustainable, not canceled.

9. *Asymmetry*

The brain physiological response to sad news or impending harm is more intense than the response to positive information.

The physiological basis of *Asymmetry* is:

"If you show subjects in neuropsychological experiments happy and sad pictures, they will spontaneously respond more strongly to the latter, as can be read in the strong deflection of the EEG" (Klein, 2006, p.27).

The feature of inequitable reactions of *pleasure* and *pain* is a consequence of human evolution. Survival is primary, and *pleasure* is secondary.

10. *Attention*

In cognitive psychology, "attention is the concentration of mental effort on sensory or mental events" (Solso, 2005, p.103).

"Our everyday experience tells us that we attend to some environmental cues more than others and that the attended cues are normally passed along for further processing, while unattended cues may not be. Which are attended to and which are not seems to stem from some control we exercise over the situation (such as looking at the instant replay to see whether the football player stepped out of bounds) and from our long-term experience (such as reading a technical report to find a certain fact). In either situation, the attention mechanism focuses on certain stimuli in preference to others, although not all of the 'extraneous' stimuli are necessarily excluded entirely from attention; they may be monitored or toned down" (Solso, 2005, p.84).

Attention has a significant effect on the *brain physiological state B(t)*. When an individual attends to an event, the event significantly influences the *brain physiological state B(t)*, while the other unattended events are excluded or toned down by the brain.

Cognitive psychology also indicates that attention is selective. "Selective attention means that at any moment we focus our awareness on only a limited aspect of all that we experience" (Myers, 2004, p.231). Selective attention results from the limited information-processing capacity of the brain.

"Many of the contemporary ideas of attention are based on the premise that there are available to the human observer a myriad of cues that surround us at any given moment. Our neurological capacity is too limited to sense all of the millions of external stimuli, but even were these stimuli detected, the brain would be unable to process all of them; our information- processing capacity is too limited" (Solso, 2005, p.83).

"In order to cope with the flood of available information, humans selectively attend to only some the cues and tune out much of the rest" (Solso, 2005, p.83).

"Selective attention is analogous to shining a flashlight in a darkened room to illuminate the things in which we are interested while keeping the other items in the dark" (Solso, 2005, p.86).

The function of *Attention* shows that the mind significantly influences the body.

The physiological basis of *Attention* is:

"When attention is directed to a single stimulus in the receptive field, there is often an increase in the firing rates of neurons that respond to the attended stimulus" (Squire, 2009, p.1122). Positron emission tomography (PET) measurements of brain activity indicate that attention activated brain regions (Corbetta, 1991, p.2383).

11. *Equivalence*

A future event that does not happen at the present time may influence the current *brain physiological state B(t)* owing to the *Equivalence Principle*.

The physiological basis of *Equivalence* is:

The human brain cannot distinguish the difference between one event that will happen in the future, and another event that is subjectively believed to happen definitely in the future, even if this event is an impossible occurrence.

Most of the features of the *brain physiological state B(t)* summarized above are based on some scientific experiments.

Chapter 3

Pleasure

The Physiological Basis of Pleasure

The physiological basis of *pleasure* can be described as follows. At any moment in time, all information from external stimuli and physiological states of the body is transferred to the brain,which undergoes conscious activities. Some information is filtered out by selective attention. In the meantime, a comparison is made between the transferred information and the information stored in memory. Changes in electrochemical activity simultaneously take place in the brain. As a result, one subjectively has a pleasant emotional experience, or a feeling of *pleasure* at the same time.

Klein described the physiological process of *pleasure* when one's needs are met. "When we're hungry, for example, there's an imbalance between the need for energy and the intake of nourishment. The body releases dynorphin, the opioid of discomfort, which is responsible for our perceiving hunger as unpleasant. An impulse is set in motion to do something against the unpleasantness. We become restless, irritable, on our guard. We look for a signal to compensate for the deficiency. We see a goal: a roast chicken! The brain releases beta-endorphin that gives a foretaste of the desired pleasure and signals that the food before us should benefit the organism. At the same time the brain very quickly releases dopamine, the molecule of desire. The circuits for wishing and wanting are closely connected. Under the influence of dopamine we become optimistic and more alert, and we make an effort to satisfy our desires. We smell the odor of meat, bite into the drumstick, and enjoy the flavor. Still more endorphin floods the brain and signals to the organism that its needs have been met and that it is returning to a state of equilibrium: it's full, and it's comfortable" (Klein, 2006, p.113).

There are the neurobiological reward and punishment systems in the brain according to neurobiology (Car, 2005, p.102). The emotional experience of *pleasure* is a by-product that is beneficial to survival and reproduction of an individual. The reward and punishment systems in the brain are beneficial for an organism to adapt to environments. "Enjoyment is a signal that the organism is getting what it needs" (Klein, 2006, p.112). "Sex is a good example: since nature wants us to pass on genetic inheritance, opioids flow at orgasm" (Klein, 2006, p.112). "Enjoyment is a signal that we are moving from a worse to a better condition" (Klein, 2006, p.113). When a *need* is satisfied, the brain produces a feeling of *pleasure* as a reward.

"In fact, animal research has revealed both a general reward system that triggers the release of the neurotransmitter dopamine and specific centers associated with the pleasures of eating, drinking, and sex. Animals, it seems, come equipped with built-in systems that reward activities essential to survival" (Myers, 2004, p.75).

Pleasure also originates from the cognitive evaluation of situations that benefit survival and reproduction. When people make cognitive evaluations of situations, the brain gives a certain type of signal. If the situation is beneficial to an individual, the brain produces a positive emotional experience. The more benefits a situation has for the individual, the more intense positive emotional experience the brain produces. For instance, having good interpersonal relationships benefits survival and reproduction of an individual. When an individual makes this cognitive evaluation, the brain produces the emotional experience of *pleasure* as a reward. Since human beings are social animals, people are interdependent. The hermetic life is not beneficial to survival and reproduction of an individual.

When the situation can harm an individual, the brain produces the emotional experience of *pain*. For example, when a person's life or property is in danger, the person will experience a feeling of *pain*. These emotional experiences of *pain* remind the person that the situation has bad consequences and some action is required to change it for the better. The more harmful the situation, the greater the intensity of the emotional experience of *pain* the brain produces.

When a person accomplishes his or her goal, the person feels very excited. Because the situation of achieving the goal is beneficial to the person's survival and reproduction or the survival of the group the person belongs to, when the person makes this type of cognitive evaluation, the brain produces a reward of *pleasure*.

Time-Dependency of Need

The term **need** in this book is not used typically as in needing something. It refers to an individual's subjective need or hope to get something, or a subjective aspiration to fulfill a desire at a certain moment or during a relatively short period of time. *Need* is defined as the sum of all subjective needs described by words such as need, want, desire, aspiration, hope, anticipation, goal, pursuit and so forth. *Need* contains the *time* factor with seconds, tens of seconds, minutes and hours as the units of time.

The term **demand** is defined in this book as the objective demands referring to something that is vital to an individual. A person's objective *demand* is not necessarily related to his or her subjective desire. For instance, the objective *demand* for oxygen is uninterrupted and continuous because survival is impossible without oxygen. There is not usually a subjective *need* for oxygen since one does not usually experience a lack of oxygen. One's subjective *need* for oxygen arises only when it is in short supply like on a high mountain peak.

In unconscious states such as deep sleep or a coma, people subjectively do not have any subjective *need*. However, one objectively *demand*s oxygen, and the appropriate temperature range for survival. Oxygen and the appropriate temperature range are objective *demands,* not subjective *needs*. When one is thirsty, one has a *need* for water. After drinking enough water, one's subjective *need* for water disappears temporarily, but the objective *demand* for water is uninterrupted and continuous.

The *State of Need* is one of the states of consciousness. There is no *need* in a state of unconsciousness.

1. Time-Dependency

There are short-term and long-term *needs* as well as cyclical *needs* such as the *needs* for food, water and sex. One's *need* is continually changing over time, and sometimes it may appear for an instant. For example, when one thinks of something, the related *need* may appear. One is not always in the *State of Need*. After one's short-term *needs* are satisfied, he or she may temporarily have no *need*, such as right after drinking, eating or having sex. If there is nothing special to do after dinner, people watch TV or read newspaper, close their eyes and relax on the sofa or remember past events, think about work or arrange their upcoming schedule. Under these circumstances, people are in the state of consciousness without any specific *need*. In states of consciousness, most of the time one is not in the *State of Need*. Even if there is a long-term *need*, one can't think of it all the time since the brain has a lot of other tasks to do.

In "Maslow's hierarchy of needs theory that there is a hierarchy of five human needs: physiological, safety, social, esteem, and self-actualization" (Robbins, 2007, p.265), but he did not consider the *time* factor. The time span of Maslow's needs is relatively long periods of time. Maslow's needs are long-term or lifetime needs. One *demands* air, water, food, and the appropriate temperature range for survival. However, our everyday experience indicates that one does not have subjective *needs* for these basics all the time. Take the *need* for food as an example, when one is hungry or sees delicious food, the *need* for food appears. After he or she has a meal and is full, there is no *need* for food for a short period of time. His or her attention tends to turn to other matters or events. But after several hours he or she may be hungry again and the *need* for food appears again. From this perspective, the *need* for food is not continuous, but cyclical. The *need* for water is also cyclical. The *need* for sex has a cyclical characteristic as well, one does not continuously think about it.

When one has a need, changes occur in his or her *brain physiological state*. For example, when one is hungry, and feels the *need* for food, changes simultaneously occur in the physiological state of one's brain.

2. *Need Intensity*

In his hierarchy of needs theory, Maslow did not consider the intensity of *need*. The intensity of one's *need* changes over time. Right after a meal, a person does not have the *need* for food. A few hours later, the person may experience a little hunger. After 10 hours, the person will be very hungry. And after 24 hours, the person will feel starvation. In other words, right after a meal, the intensity of *need* for food can be considered as zero. As time passes, one starts feeling a little bit hungry. And then, the degree of feeling hungry will increase step by step and the intensity of *need* for food will gradually increase. The **Need Intensity** for food 24 hours after the meal is greater than the *Need*

Intensity 12 hours after the meal.

3. Specific *Need*

In addition to basic *needs*, people have many other specific *needs* in daily life. For example, people may want to do a lot of other things such as buying a new cell phone, traveling, watching a movie, going to beauty salon, joining a training course or finishing a project.

How does a specific *need* arise? Some *needs* originate from physiological *demands*. For example, when we're hungry, we *need* something to eat. When we're thirsty, we *need* water to drink. *Need* also has social characteristics, and arises from society. For instance, after viewing a clothing advertisement, there is a desire to buy the clothes. After seeing a friend's new cell phone, one wants to buy a new phone. A picture of Niagara Falls can spur the desire to travel. Watching an erotic film can create the desire for sex. People tend to compare themselves to each other or have a desire to imitate, like those who strive to have all of the material goods that their neighbors have. After old *needs* are satisfied, new ones may arise. In other words, lots of specific *needs* arise from the influence of the surrounding environment.

In the *States of Thinking, Remembering the Past, Imagining the Future,* if people think of some things that they hope to obtain, the *need* arises.

Many *needs* can be satisfied within a short period of time. Some can be satisfied after a long period. Yet some *needs* will not be satisfied even in an entire life.

Sources of Pleasure

There are many sources of *pleasure*. The major sources of *pleasure* produced within seconds or tens of seconds are discussed and summarized in detail below.

1. Satisfaction of *Need*

Within a short period of time in the process of satisfying *needs*, one can feel the emotional experience of *pleasure*. The more intense the need, the stronger the *pleasure* originated from satisfying the need.

For example, drinking water will satisfy thirst. When we're hungry, comfort comes from eating and erasing the negative feeling of hunger. On a hot day, going into an air-conditioned room will satisfy the *need* for a comfortable temperature. After a college application process, a student received an acceptance letter from his or her top choice of universities, he or she feels very excited. After buying a lottery ticket, a person is waiting for the announcement of results. At the moment the person learns he or she has won big, the desire to make money is satisfied, and he or she feels overwhelming pleased.

Satisfying one's *need* is a major source of *pleasure*, but not the only one. After one's *need* is satisfied, the feeling of *pleasure* begins to weaken and eventually vanishes. A satisfied *need* does not contribute to *pleasure* any longer.

2. Cognitive Evaluations

People can experience *pleasure* in the cognitive process. Relying on their values, people make subjective evaluations of situations or events. When the situations or events are beneficial to them, people may experience *pleasure* from the evaluations.

Some types of cognitive evaluations are described as follows:

(1) Within a short period of time, cognitive evaluation of past events

For example, when the evaluative result about their quality of life during a past period is positive, people probably feel pleased when answering a survey of happiness.

(2) Within a short period of time, cognitive evaluation of the current circumstances

If the circumstances are beneficial to a person, the evaluation may produce positive emotional experiences. For example, a chess player in the middle-stage of the game has a positive feeling when he feels he is going to win after evaluating the circumstances on the board.

(3) Within a short period of time, cognitive evaluation of the current career or work

If a person thinks what he or she does is meaningful and valuable, the person usually feels good about it. For example, if a person strongly believes that the true value of life is helping others, then he or she will feel content or pleased after helping someone.

(4) Within a short period of time, *social comparison* with others (Carr, 2005, p.48)

"*Social comparison.* The process of comparing oneself to others. Downward social comparisons (with those worse off than ourselves) increase happiness but upward social comparisons (with those better off than ourselves) decrease happiness" (Carr, 2005, p.48).

When comparing oneself with others, a person may be pleased after evaluating and finding his or her circumstances to be better in comparison. For instance, when a man compares himself with his former classmates and realizes that his social status and income are relatively high, he can be very pleased and content.

(5) Within a short period of time, cognitive evaluation of the future

When a person evaluates his or her future and subjectively considers that the future is bright and brilliant, the person probably has a positive feeling.

(6) The times when people have made some progress or achieved some intermediate-stage goals

People set a number of long-term goals in different stages based on their values. In the process of moving toward these goals, people have made some progress on the way. At this time, upon seeing the favorable result from cognitive evaluations conducted, they will naturally feel glad. For example, suppose the goal is climbing a mountain peak. People will feel pleased when they reach the halfway point towards the mountain peak.

3. Goal Attainment

When people attain the goals they have set, they feel very excited and happy. This is like winning a gold medal at the Olympic Games, for example.

4. Aesthetic Process

"I am talking about the curious fact that, on my evening walks with Willie during the long Minnesota winters, I can get real sensuous pleasure form looking at the trees, their leafless branches making beautiful and complex patterns against the evening sky" (Lykken, 1999, p.28). "Much more certain than any of these speculations is the fact that our species, for reasons that are as yet inscrutable, derives joy from music, from the beauties of nature or of human art, and from the gifted use of words in poetry or prose" (Lykken, 1999, p.30).

5. Satisfaction of Curiosity

Within a short period of time, the process of satisfying a person's curiosity can produce the emotional experience of *pleasure*. The reason why most people like sightseeing is that their curiosity about a location or a culture is satisfied.

Curiosity is human nature. "There is ample evidence that people and animals seek novel and informative stimulation; consciousness seems to have a preference for 'news'. Repetitive, predictable, 'old' stimuli tend to fade from consciousness regardless of their sensory modality, degree of abstractness, or physical intensity. *Novelty* can defined as change in the physical environment (dishabituation), disconfirmation of expectation (surprise), or violation of skilled routines" (Solso, 2005, p.155). "That's just what curiosity does well—enabling us not just to accept new things but also to want them" (Klein, 2006, p.99).

The major function of curiosity is to enhance the ability to perceive new information. The environment for human survival is complicated and can change quickly. Curiosity enables an individual to subtly perceive all the changes and take prompt measures. Individuals who can avoid danger effectively have more chances of survival. In the long process of evolution, those who were more curious had a better chance of survival, while those without curiosity died out. This is why the majority of people existing in the world constantly pursue new experiences and knowledge.

When one's curiosity is satisfied, the brain produces a reward of *pleasure*, which motivates interest in new things.

When a person has sufficient shelter, food and clothing, he or she temporarily does not face any crisis of survival and reproduction. At this time, if the person does not pursue gaining new information or new things and does not make some preparations for future survival and reproduction, the brain may produce negative emotional experiences such as boredom or empty feelings.

Curiosity is a human characteristic that is beneficial to survival and reproduction.

6. Gambling

People can experience *pleasure* when they gamble and win. Gambling is human nature. The passion for gambling indicates that humans have the propensity to "do nothing and get something" or "work less and get more". When a gambler wins, he or she spends relatively little and gains relatively more. It is beneficial to survival and reproduction. So, the brain produces an experience of *pleasure* as a reward.

But when a gambler loses, the gambler loses what he or she had. It is not good for survival and reproduction. In this case, the brain produces an emotional experience of *pain* as a punishment.

7. *Flow* Experience

"*Flow* activities allow a person to focus on goals that are clear and compatible" (Csikszentmihalyi, 1997, p.30).

"These exceptional moments are what I have called *flow experiences*. The metaphor of 'flow' is one that many people have used to describe the sense of effortless action they feel in moments that stand out as the best in their lives. Athletes refer to it as 'being in the zone,' religious mystics as being in 'ecstasy,' artists and musicians as aesthetic rapture" (Csikszentmihalyi, 1997, p.29).

"When we are in flow, we are not happy" (Csikszentmihalyi, 1997, p.32). "Only after the task is completed do we then have the leisure to look back on what has happened, and then we are flooded with gratitude for the excellence of that experience - then, in retrospect, we are happy" (Csikszentmihalyi, 1997, p.32).

8. *State of Thinking*

In the process of judging, abstracting, reasoning, imagining, and problem solving, one usually does not experience a feeling of *pleasure*. A person can experience *pleasure* only after finding out a solution for a problem.

9. *State of Remembering the Past*

One may experience a feeling of *pleasure* when one

remembers pleasant events that happened in the past, such as the event of winning a lottery many years ago.

10. *State of Imagining the Future*

One may experience a feeling of *pleasure* when one imagines or expects good future events that do not happen for the time being. For example, after receiving a new job offer, a person feels quite happy when he or she thinks about starting the new job in two weeks earning a better salary.

11. *State of Meditation*

One may experience a feeling of *pleasure* when he or she is in the *State of Meditation*.

"Meditation, for example, is controlled perception that enables us to lose ourselves and experience euphoria. When a Zen monk counts his breathing, when a Yogi repeats his mantra, or when a Christian is lost in prayer—the person meditating always directs his perception towards a simple focus. In this way he occupies his brain, prevents it from turning to everyday cares, calms his mind, and relaxes his body" (Klein, 2006, p.226). "Many people who do practice the discipline of meditation experience a kind of quiet joy as soon as their thoughts have come to rest" (Klein, 2006, p.226).

"There is a large body of scientific evidence to show that meditation, which involves this process, has a positive effect on immediate and long-term psychological well-being for a wide range of healthy people and also those with physical and mental health difficulties" (Carr, 2005, p.219).

"A physician who conducts stress research at the

University of Pennsylvania and has been practicing Buddhist meditation for thirty years, describes such a moment as follows: 'There was a feeling of energy centered within me...going out to infinite space and returning ...There was a relaxing of the dualistic mind, and an intense feeling of love...clarity, transparency and joy. I felt a deep and profound sense of connection to everything, recognizing that there never was a true separation at all" (Klein, 2006, p.227).

12. Drugs

Psychoactive drugs can produce the emotional experiences of *pleasure* for a short period of time.

13. Other Factors

The other factors that are not included above can lead to the emotional experiences of *pleasure*.

In the above items 8, 9, 10 and 11, only conscious activities in the brain can produce the emotional experiences of *pleasure* without any external stimulation. As Csikszentmihalyi pointed out, "A person can make himself happy, or miserable, regardless of what is actually happening 'outside', just by changing the contents of consciousness" (Csikszentmihalyi, 1990, p.24).

Different kinds of *pleasures* from different sources cannot replace each other. The *pleasure* produced by satisfying one's appetite can't be replaced by the *pleasure* produced by satisfying one's sexual desire.

There are no strict boundaries in the classification of

pleasure sources. Some of them may overlap and repeat each other. For instance, the process of satisfying *needs* includes cognitive evaluation. The Aesthetic process also includes cognitive evaluation. The aim of this classification is to analyze the sources of *pleasure* from different perspectives.

Features of Pleasure Intensity

The term **Pleasure Intensity** is defined as the strength of a positive feeling or emotion an individual experiences at any moment in time.

Pleasure Intensity $P = P(t)$, which is a function of time t.

$P(t)$ is a psychological magnitude representing an individual's subjective experience. At any moment t, the intensity of subjective *pleasure* is positively related to $P(t)$.

$P > 0$ stands for *pleasure*, $P < 0$ stands for *pain*, $P = 0$ stands for neither *pleasure* nor *pain*.

The features of *Pleasure Intensity* are summarized in figure 3.1 based on the features of the *brain physiological state*.

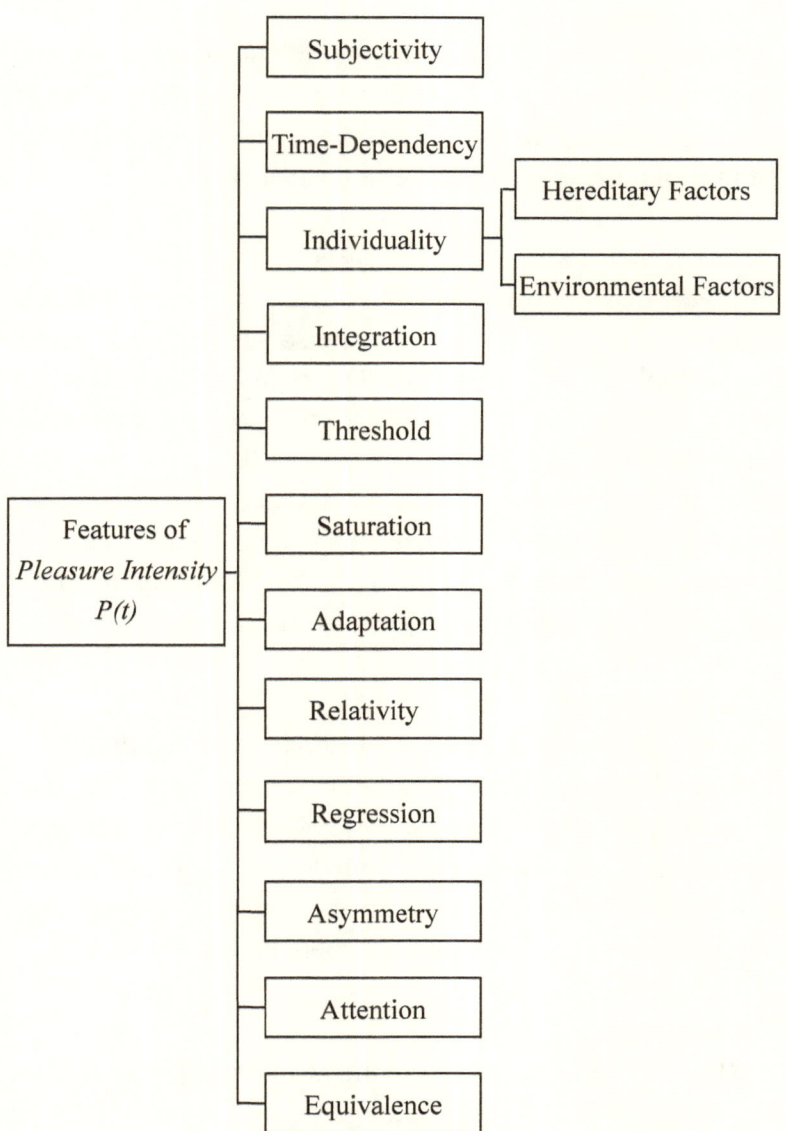

Figure 3.1 Features of *Pleasure Intensity*

1. *Subjectivity*

Pleasure Intensity is the strength of subjective emotional experience. Relative to objectivity, the *Subjectivity* of *Pleasure Intensity* stresses the subjectivity of psychological feelings, not the objective criteria for *pleasure*.

2. *Time-Dependency*

Pleasure Intensity originating from the same external stimulation differs for the same person at different times. For example, in the process of the cognitive evaluation, an individual experiences *pleasure* from a positive evaluation. After the cognitive evaluation, the individual's attention turns to other matters or events, the *pleasure* originating from the cognitive evaluation disappears. Similarly, states of consciousness such as the *State of Remembering the Past* and *State of Imagining the Future* are all time-dependent.

3. *Individuality*

Each individual's brain is different. Each individual's *Pleasure Intensity* in response to the same external stimulus is also different. Relative to other individuals, the *Individuality* of *Pleasure Intensity* stresses differences between individuals. For example, some individuals may feel anger in some situations but others may not.

4. *Integration*

Pleasure Intensity at any moment in time is a product of the interaction of all external stimuli and internal physiological factors, as well as the state of consciousness at that moment. For example, a person with stomachache is having dinner with friends. While eating and talking, the person is informed about his or her winning a lottery prize, at the same time he or she feels a little pain in the stomach. His or her subjective emotional experience at this moment is the product of the interaction of the stomachache, the food stimulus, the informational stimulus and what his or her attention is focused on.

5. *Threshold*

Internal stimuli and external stimuli can make contributions to *Pleasure Intensity* only when these stimuli exceed their thresholds. Some thresholds change over time. *Threshold* also has a feature of *Adaptation*. After repetition of one stimulus, the threshold of this stimulus for an individual will increase.

Suppose that a person with a $3,000 monthly income wins a $10 prize, the person may not feel pleased. The person feels pleased only when he or she wins $300. This means the person's money stimulation threshold is $300. Further suppose, this person wins $300 prize a few times in a month, he or she is increasingly less pleased. The person can not feel pleased again until he or she wins $400. In other words, after being stimulated a few times, the person's money stimulation threshold increases by about 33%.

Suppose again, that this person wins $300 in a month and he or she feels glad, but in the next month, he or she gets a pay rise and earns $4,000 a month. He or she can feel glad only when the amount of winnings is $400 or more. That is, the increase of income also increases the person's money stimulation threshold.

Different external stimuli have their own thresholds. For example, the measuring unit of the drug stimulation threshold is different from the unit of money stimulation threshold.

Sometimes when a *need* is satisfied, if the level of satisfaction does not exceed the threshold of *pleasure*, a person can not experience *pleasure*. For example, during a chess game, a player wants to take a rook of the opponent. This is a short-term *need*. After a while, the player takes the opponent's rook, but loses a knight simultaneously. The net benefit does not exceed *pleasure* threshold. This person does not have a feeling of *pleasure*.

Sometimes the result of cognitive evaluation is satisfactory, but when the level of satisfaction does not exceed the threshold of *pleasure*, one does not have the experience of *pleasure*.

There is a threshold of respect by others. If one is respected by those in a lower social class, the person will probably not feel *pleasure*. But if respected by his or her peers or people in a higher class, the person is more likely to feel *pleasure*.

The threshold of sex also changes over time. Without sexual intercourse for a long time, the sexual threshold decreases, the *need* for sex increases, the satisfaction of sexual intercourse makes a greater contribution to *pleasure* under this circumstance.

Shortly after sexual desire has been satisfied, the *need* for sex decreases, the threshold of sex increases and one needs stronger sex stimulus to achieve the same level of *pleasure*. For example, shortly after a sexual intercourse, a man needs more beautiful or younger woman to evoke him to get the same sexual urges as before.

The *Threshold* of *Pleasure Intensity* is closely connected to the *Threshold* of the *brain physiological state.*

6. *Saturation*

When the external stimulation intensity gradually increases, people experience a gradual increase in the level of *pleasure*. But when external stimulation intensity increases to a certain magnitude (saturation level), the level of *pleasure* people experience no longer increases. *Pleasure Intensity* reaches its limit, and the experience of *pleasure* reaches the state of *saturation.*

Imagine a person with a monthly income of $3,000 respectively won lottery prizes of $10, $100, $1 thousand, $10 thousands, $100 thousands, $1 million and $10 millions. At the beginning, with the increased amount of each prize, the level of excitement increased. But when the amount reached 1 million, the level of excitement reached the limit of the brain physiological response. The level of excitement of winning 1 million was at the same level of excitement as winning 10 millions.

For the same external stimulation, the saturation level changes over time. Suppose, a man had a monthly income of $3,000 and his saturation level for money stimulation was $1 million. After a decade of efforts, he had a successful business, and his annual income reached $500 thousands. At this time, the saturation level for money stimulation was not $1 million. It could take 500 millions to get him excited and reach the limit of the brain physiological response.

Different external stimuli have their own saturation levels. For example, the measuring unit of drug stimulation saturation level is different from the unit of money stimulation saturation level.

The *Saturation* of *Pleasure Intensity* is closely connected to the *Saturation* of the *brain physiological state* because the physiological responses in the human brain to external stimulation are limited.

7. Adaptation

There are two implications for the *Adaptation* of *Pleasure Intensity*.

(1) *Diminishing marginal Pleasure Intensity*

Because the brain's response to external stimulation is *diminishing marginal response*, *Pleasure Intensity* originated from external stimulation is also ***diminishing marginal Pleasure Intensity***.

Additional increments of the external stimulus intensity to the brain, within some stated period of time, will yield smaller and smaller increments of *Pleasure Intensity*.

For example, when we're hungry, the first slice of bread tastes great. The third slice is less delicious than the first, and the fifth slice is less tasty than the third. At the physiological level, *diminishing marginal Pleasure Intensity* originates from the sensory suppression effect (Squire, 2009, p.1129) of the human nervous system that has a mechanism to compress the range of external physical stimulation (Gleitman, 1987, p.116).

Diminishing marginal Pleasure Intensity is closely connected to *diminishing marginal response* of the *brain physiological state.*

(2) *Adaptation*

In the words of Myers (2005, p.655), "The adaptation-level phenomenon implies that feelings of success and failure, satisfaction and dissatisfaction, are relative to prior achievements. If our current achievements fall below what we previously accomplished, we feel dissatisfied, frustrated; if they rise above that level, we feel successful, satisfied. If we continue to achieve, however, we soon adapt to success. What formerly felt good registers as neutral, and what formerly felt neutral now feels like deprivation. Most of us have experienced the adaptation-level phenomenon. More consumer goods, academic achievement, or social prestige provide an initial surge of pleasure. Yet all too soon the feeling wanes. Then we need an even higher level to give us another surge of pleasure".

Alan Carr explained the reasons for *Adaptation*. "We have evolved in a way that we are designed to quickly habituate or adapt to situations that give us pleasure because it was adaptive for our hunting and gathering ancestors. People who quickly habituated to the pleasure of any gains they made in obtaining better food or shelter were naturally selected. Those who rested on their laurels for a long time on each occasion when they achieved a goal that entailed the experience of long-lasting pleasure did not survive" (Carr, 2005, p.35).

The *Adaptation* of *Pleasure Intensity* is closely connected to the *Adaptation* of the *brain physiological state.*

8. *Relativity*

Relativity is also called *social comparisons* (Carr, 2005, p.35). "Much of life revolves around social comparisons" (Myers, 2005, p.44).

"Our level of happiness is influenced by how we rate ourselves and our current circumstances, not only in comparison with our recent circumstances, but also in comparison with those of others. We compare ourselves with other people in terms of health, personal attractiveness and that of our partners and children, wealth, social status, academic and athletic achievement, and so forth. This process of social comparison in ancestral times was adaptive because it led us to strive to be the best and to have the best resources in our group and so propagate our genetic line" (Carr, 2005, p.35).

"Happiness, too, is relative not only to our past experience but also to our comparisons with others. Whether we feel good or bad depends on with whom we're comparing ourselves" (Myers, 2005, p.656).

In society, sometimes people who have no direct relationship to us, such as major shareholders of listed companies, successful entrepreneurs, movie stars, etc., can influence our *happiness*, but the degree of this kind of influence is limited.

The term ***Similar Reference Group*** defined in this book refers to a group of people who are similar to us in age, education, etc. (especially those of the same gender), who are proximal to us, who are people we have direct contact with, such as our brothers and sisters, classmates, relatives, colleagues, peers, friends and acquaintances. People in

Similar Reference Group have significant influences on the level of our *happiness*.

The *Relativity* of *Pleasure Intensity* is closely connected to the *Relativity* of the *brain physiological state*.

9. Regression

"Brickman and Campbell coined the term 'hedonic treadmill' to describe this process of rapid adaptation whereby people react strongly to both positive and negative recent events with sharp increases or decreases in happiness but in most instances return to their happiness set-point over relatively short periods of time" (Carr, 2005, p.35).

After a *need* is met, the feeling of *pleasure* disappears. "Desire and enjoyment are closely connected, but they are also opposed to one another" (Klein, 2006, p.116). "As soon as everything is back in order, the sense of pleasure dissipates" (Klein, 2006, p.113). "Our emotions tend to balance around normal" (Myers, 2004, p.527). "Over the long ride, our emotional ups and downs tend to balance" (Myers, 2004, p.523).

The *Regression* of *Pleasure Intensity* is closely connected to the *Regression* of the *brain physiological state*.

10. Asymmetry

Asymmetry refers to inequitable reactions of *pleasure* and *pain*. "We are also designed in evolutionary terms so that losses lead to more intense emotional experiences than gains of the same magnitude, because this was adaptive for our ancestors. So, loss of an animal that had been hunted long and hard and got away led to a far more intense emotional experience than that associated with successfully killing the same animal after a long chase. Those who experienced intense emotions following loss were strongly motivated to work hard to avoid loss and so survived. Those that did not experience intense emotions in response to loss were not motivated to work hard to avoid loss and probably experienced multiple losses of food, shelter and other things necessary for survival and so died out. In modern times, this legacy remains with us. The despair experienced at losing €100 is not matched in magnitude by the satisfaction of earning or winning €100. One outcome of being designed in this way by the process of natural selection is that to achieve intense satisfaction a great deal must be acquired. However, to experience intense distress, only a little needs to be lost. Both of these factors compromise our capacity for happiness. Furthermore our disappointment at the small increments in happiness that arise from big gains and the large decrements in happiness entailed by small losses may future detract from our happiness" (Carr, 2005, pp.36-37).

"Generally, we experience negative feelings more intensely and more readily than positive ones" (Klein, 2006, p.27). "Our systems are skewed more to the experience of unhappiness than to the enjoyment of pleasure, and we perceive annoyance and discouragement more quickly and strongly than we do joy" (Klein, 2006, p.28).

The *Asymmetry* of *Pleasure Intensity* is closely connected to the *Asymmetry* of the *brain physiological state.*

11. *Attention*

The brain only processes the attended information, and weakens or tunes out the rest.

When an individual focuses his or her attention on an event, the event significantly influences the *Pleasure Intensity*, while the other unattended events are excluded or toned down by the brain.

When an individual's attention is focused on a certain factor, the threshold of this factor decreases to minimum, and the thresholds of other factors increase. For example, when playing in a close chess tournament, players can go for hours without feeling hungry (since their attention is not focused on food, the threshold of food stimulation is high during this period of time). But when they are reminded about eating or they see food (when their attention is focused on food, the threshold of food stimulation decreases at this moment), they immediately feel hungry.

At any moment, whether a love, or a satisfied *need*, or a cognitive evaluation makes a major contribution to the experience of *pleasure* depends on what attention is focused on. If an individual's attention is focused on love, love makes a major contribution to the emotional experience at this moment, the other factors are weakened or excluded by the brain. If an individual's attention is focused on a cognitive evaluation, the result of the cognitive evaluation makes a major contribution to the emotional experience, the other factors are weakened or excluded by the brain.

In daily life, the brain's attention is constantly changing over time. An individual's attention can be focused on one factor for a long time, or for a moment.

The *Attention* of *Pleasure Intensity* is closely connected to the *Attention* of the *brain physiological state*.

12. *Equivalence*

A perceived future event that does not happen at the present time may influence an individual's current emotional experiences and cognitive evaluations according to the *Equivalence Principle*.

The *Equivalence* of *Pleasure Intensity* is closely connected to the *Equivalence* of the *brain physiological state*.

Features in the above classification may overlap and repeat. This kind of classification aims primarily to analyze the features of *Pleasure Intensity* from different perspectives.

The features of *Pleasure Intensity* are closely connected to the features of the *brain physiological state*. In other words, the features of *Pleasure Intensity* are indirectly associated with some scientific experimental results and directly come from the statistical results of surveys.

Within a time interval of tens of seconds, some factors are seemingly irrelevant to *Pleasure Intensity*. However they implicitly influence *Pleasure Intensity*. One type of implicit factors such as age, gender, personality traits and so forth is connected to hereditary factors. The other type of implicit factors such as culture, education, values, religion, ethics, and so forth is connected to environmental factors. These factors are contained in the physical brain.

Within a time interval of tens of seconds, factors such as

wealth, social status, love, affection, safety, freedom, democracy, equality and interpersonal relationships, can make contributions to *Pleasure Intensity*. Which factor makes a major contribution to *Pleasure Intensity* depends on what one's attention is focused on during that period of time.

Three Categories of Emotional States

Emotional states taking place during a short period of time can be approximately grouped into three categories.

(1) **Pleasure State**: a person subjectively has emotional experiences of *pleasure*.

(2) **Pain State**: a person subjectively has emotional experiences of *pain*.

(3) **Neutral State**: a person subjectively has neither *pleasure* nor *pain* emotional experiences.

In daily life, people in a waking state are involved in certain kinds of activities which can include some or all states of consciousness such as *State of Need, State of Pleasure, State of Cognition, State of Thinking, State of Remembering the Past, State of Imagining the Future,* and *State of Meditation.* Activities include doing a job, completing tasks, watching television, doing housework, playing tennis, doing exercises, chatting, flying on a plane, imagining something, remembering past events, solving problems and so forth.

In the process of ordinary activities, people may not have a specific *need*, but may also create a new *need*. This kind of short-term *need* can be changed or cancelled at any time. In the process of an activity, sometimes even if one's *need* is satisfied, but the level of satisfaction does not exceed the *pleasure* threshold, the person can not experience *pleasure*.

While engaged in an activity, people often make cognitive evaluations. Whether or not they experience *pleasure* depends on if the results of overall evaluations are beneficial to them, and if the net benefit of the evaluations exceeds the *pleasure* threshold. Even if the results from the overall evaluations are beneficial to them, as long as the net benefit does not exceed the *pleasure* threshold, they can not experience *pleasure*.

In the process of an activity, whether or not an external stimulus can make people feel *pleasure* depends on if the stimulus is beneficial to them, and if the net benefit exceeds the *pleasure* threshold. Even if the external stimulus is beneficial to them, as long as the net benefit does not exceed *pleasure* threshold, they can not experience *pleasure*.

In general, most of the time in life, people are in a neutral emotional state in which they do not have either *pleasure* or *pain* experiences.

"What we do during an average day can be divided into three major kinds of activities" (Csikszentmihalyi, 1997, p.10).

(1) Productive Activities: working at work, or studying. "The first and largest includes what we must do in order to generate energy for survival and comfort. Nowadays this is almost synonymous with 'making money', since money has

become the medium of exchange for most things. However, for young people still in school, learning might be included among these productive activities, because for them education is the equivalent of adult work, and the first will lead into the second" (Csikszentmihalyi, 1997, p.10).

(2) Maintenance Activities: eating, cooking, cleaning, shopping, housework, washing up, dressing, driving, transportation, and so forth (Csikszentmihalyi, 1997, p.9).

(3) Leisure Activities: reading, watching TV, socializing, doing sports, listening to music, talking to friends, doing a hobby, getting involved in exercise, playing a musical instrument, or going out to a movie or restaurant (Csikszentmihalyi, 1997, pp.9-39), surfing the internet and so forth.

How daily activities influence *pleasure* is analyzed below.

1. Productive Activities and *Pleasure*

In the process of working, each case should be analyzed based on the specific circumstance. When people focus their attention on what they are doing, or on a task they are performing, they do not feel *pleasure*, because to experience *pleasure* they must focus on their inner states, and that would take away attention from the task at hand. For example, when racing, the driver's attention is totally focused on driving. When a chef is engrossed in cooking; a pianist concentrates on playing a challenging musical composition; a teacher is immersed in explaining a lesson; a surgeon concentrates on a demanding operation, their attention is totally focused on the tasks at hand. In the process of these activities, they usually do not have experiences of *pleasure*. Only after the tasks are completed, and when they evaluate the results as positive, do they experience *pleasure*. If people encounter some obstacles in the process of working, or something goes wrong with it, they may feel irritated and angry. If everything goes smoothly, people have made some progress or achieved some intermediate-stage goals, they are likely to feel pleasant. If people face danger in the process of completing a certain task, they may have emotional experiences of *pain*.

In the process of studying and acquiring knowledge, if the new knowledge is relatively difficult to master, the process does not produce *pleasure*. On the contrary, it may produce *pain*. It can produce a feeling of *pleasure* when people have made some progress or achieved some intermediate-stage goals, or when they evaluate the results as positive after mastering the new knowledge, or when they anticipate good returns in the future owing to mastering new knowledge or skills.

The process of talking to strangers such as shop assistants, flight attendants, government clerks, waiters, barbers and so forth, usually does not produce *pleasure*. Doing a certain thing such as buying a ticket or applying for a visa usually does not produce *pleasure*. Only after the action is successfully completed and the evaluative results are positive, is a person likely to have a feeling of *pleasure*.

Whether or not people experience *pleasure* in the process of activities such as reading documents, presenting at a meeting, having a discussion, listening to a report, or listening to a lecture depends on if the information perceived is beneficial to them, and if the net benefit exceeds the *pleasure* threshold.

In the process of addressing a report, teaching, making a speech, taking exams, doing homework, reciting, typing and so forth, people have to concentrate on what they are doing. Otherwise, they are not able to finish the task. The process of these activities usually does not produce *pleasure*. Only after these things are completed, and people evaluate the results as positive, can they have a feeling of *pleasure*.

2. Maintenance Activities and *Pleasure*

The process of dressing up, taking a shower, brushing teeth, getting a haircut and so forth usually does not produce either *pleasure* or *pain*. Commuting to work usually does not make people feel *pleasure* or *pain* either (Being held up in traffic jam sometimes may produce *pain*). When people are hungry, eating food is a type of joy. However, if people often eat the same food, the stimulus evoked by the food does not exceed the *pleasure* threshold, and they can not experience *pleasure*.

In the process of eating, people do not experience *pleasure* all the time. At the moment when one is almost full, the food-related *pleasure* threshold increases and additional food is unlikely to produce any marked feelings of *pleasure*.

Doing housework usually is not enjoyable for most of us. When people buy a needed item at a reasonable price, they usually feel neither *pleasure* nor *pain*. Sometimes people encounter queues, traffic jams, or inflated prices when shopping, they may feel unsatisfactory and annoyed. People may feel glad when they have bought things they like very much at a lower price than expected.

When excretion is a very urgent need, a person can feel relief and comfort in the process of excretion. When a person has a need of excretion and that is not urgent, if the person goes to a washroom and excretes right away, he or she may not feel relief. Then the process of excretion is neutral, neither *pleasure* nor *pain.*

3. Leisure Activities and *Pleasure*

If stimulation from the information people get in the process of reading newspapers, watching television, or surfing the internet does not exceed the *pleasure* threshold, they can not have a feeling of *pleasure.* Neutral information that is neither beneficial nor harmful to people does not contribute to *pleasure.* The information that is beneficial to them can contribute to *pleasure.* The information that is harmful to them contributes to *pain.* In most cases when people read newspapers, watch television and surf the internet, they get information that is neutral. Thus, people usually are in the *Neutral State* in the process of the media consumption.

When people do what they like, the feeling of *pleasure* is likely to last longer. When playing a game or taking part in a competition, one is not delighted if the challenges are too low relative to one's skills. If the challenges are too high one gets frustrated. Only when the challenges are matched with one's skills, is one likely to be delighted after winning.

Whether or not we feel *pleasure* in the process of talking privately to persons we know (family members, relatives, friends, acquaintances and colleagues) depends on the feedback. When they react positively to what is said and the benefit from the feedback exceeds the *pleasure* threshold, we feel pleased. If the feedback is negative, then we may feel angry or hurt. If the feedback is neutral, we do not experience *pleasure* or *pain*.

During noncompetitive physical exercises, the brain releases chemical substances making people feel comfortable after exercise. "In the short term exercise induces positive mood states and in the long term regular exercise leads to greater happiness. The short-term effects of exercise are due to the fact that exercise leads to the release of endorphins, morphine-like chemical substances produced in the brain. The longer-term increases in happiness associated with exercise are due to the fact that regular exercise reduces depression and anxiety, enhances the speed and accuracy of our work, improves our self-concepts, promotes fitness and leads to better cardiovascular functioning. Regular exercise also slows down or prevents weight gain with ageing. Regular exercise throughout adulthood reduces the risk of heart disease and cancer and is associated with longevity" (Carr, 2005, p. 32).

Whether or not people experience *pleasure* in the process of competitive physical activities depends on the evaluation of the existing situation and on the anticipated results. In other words, it depends on whether the result of overall evaluation is positive, and whether the level of benefit exceeds the *pleasure* threshold.

People may experience *pleasure* during traveling, when their curiosity is satisfied, and moreover, when the level of satisfaction exceeds the *pleasure* threshold.

Whether or not people feel *pleasure* while gambling, depends on how much they win and whether the level of winning exceeds their *pleasure* thresholds.

Whether or not people experience *pleasure* while listening to music, watching television or a film depends on if the external information received exceeds the *pleasure* threshold.

If a person is not occupied during leisure time, he or she may feel lazy, bored, lonely or empty. When people idle or daydream, whether or not they have a feeling of *pleasure* depends on what they think about and if it exceeds the *pleasure* threshold during this process.

If love can be grouped into the following four states, the emotional experiences are different in different states.

The initial state: When people begin to select, get to know each other, and evaluate each other, there is no *pleasure* normally (except for love at first sight).

The state of falling in love: The *need* for love is partially or fully satisfied, and one feels extreme *pleasure*.

The honeymoon state: The *need* for love is partially or fully satisfied and one is extremely excited and feels *pleasure* intensively.

The lovelorn state: The *need* for love can not be satisfied. One feels extreme *pain* resulted from recent break up or loss of love.

As can be seen from the above analyses, people who are engaged in three kinds of activities are normally in the *Neutral State* most of the time. There are at least two reasons for this conclusion. One is that their attention is focused on the activities that they are involved in. The other is that even if these activities are accompanied with factors such as remembering, thinking, judging, abstracting, reasoning, imagining, and a *need* being created and satisfied, but the level of satisfaction does not exceed the *pleasure* threshold, the brain does not produce emotional experiences of *pleasure*.

Chapter 4

Happiness

Features of Happiness

The previous chapter illustrated the features of *Pleasure Intensity* within a shorter period of time. In this chapter, two important features of *happiness* during a longer period of time are proposed.

1. *Preference of Attention*

(1) **Preference of Attention** means that attention is not equally allocated to every stimulus or event.

(2) Attention tends to be directed to deficiencies, or unfavorable factors. People tend to focus their attention on factors related to their survival and reproduction. Events or factors related to people's survival and reproduction usually take precedence.

(3) People tend to pay more attention to the future than the past, because future events can more significantly influence people's survival and reproduction than past events.

There are many kinds of factors associated with survival and reproduction. Those that are vital factors or pressing needs related to survival or reproduction of people get the most attention. The more dangerous or harmful the event is to survival or reproduction, the more attention is focused on it.

There are many kinds of human *needs*. If a *need* is not met, attention is directed to it and often stays there owing to the *Preference of Attention*. Then this *need* has a great impact on *happiness* during the period. When there are several *needs* that are not met, attention is directed to the most urgent *need* for survival.

The *Preference of Attention* is an important feature that is beneficial to individuals' survival and reproduction. Survival and reproduction are primary, *pleasure* and *happiness* are secondary.

2. *Wooden Barrel Principle*

In economics, the ***Wooden Barrel Principle*** (LI, 1994, p.85) refers to a wooden barrel where the shortest plank of wood determines the amount of water held in the barrel.

There are many factors related to survival and reproduction. There are also many kinds of human *needs*. If we consider each factor that influences survival or reproduction and each human *need* as a plank of a wooden barrel, then the level of *happiness* in a lifetime of an individual is determined by the height and the duration of the short planks.

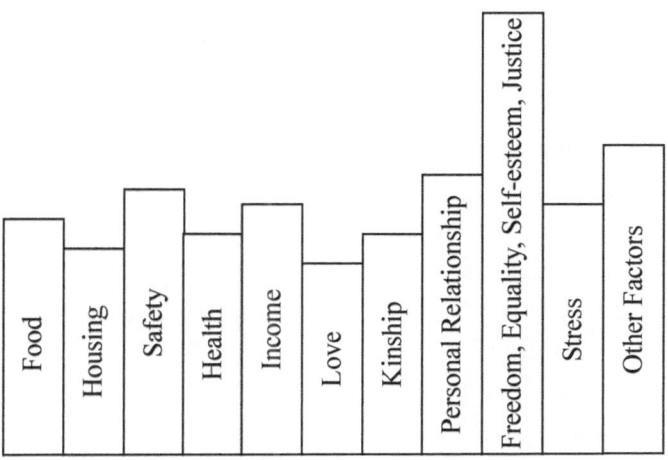

Figure 4.1 Schematic Diagram of the *Wooden Barrel Principle*

At any moment in time, the attended factors or events have the greatest impact on the feeling of *pleasure* at that moment. Owing to the *Preference of Attention,* attention stays on those deficient factors for a longer period of time. People often put their attention on the short planks instinctively, and experience the *pleasure* or *pain* from the short planks. For example, parents are usually most concerned about the child who is in the worst situation. In this case the child has the greatest impact on the level of the parents' *happiness*.

If a person has a very painful "plank" such as being lovelorn, then his or her attention is often stuck on it for a long period of time, from which he or she experiences the *pain*. In the meantime, the other long planks of *pleasure* factors, such as wealth or social status, are unnoticed most of the time and remain idle during this period.

After the problem of the shortest plank is solved, the second shortest plank automatically becomes the new shortest plank. For example, when an individual is often hungry, and has poor living conditions, the first problem for him or her to be solved is to have enough to eat and food shortage is the shortest plank. When the problem of food shortage is solved, poor living conditions will become the new shortest plank.

If the shortest plank problem of poor living conditions is solved, then there will be a new shortest plank. For example, a man moves into a bigger apartment and his living conditions are improved. But his neighborhood changes too, that is, some people in his *Similar Reference Group* change. If most people in his neighborhoods have a car and he doesn't, a new *need* will probably arise. A pressing *need* of having his own car may become his new shortest plank.

Three Factors Influencing Happiness

Borrowing the concept from Herzberg's Two-factor Theory (Robbins, 2007, p.267) in management, factors that influence *happiness* for long periods of time are classified into three categories.

1. *Essential Factors*
The term *Essential Factors* defined in this book refer to the factors that are more related to *pain*. Without these

factors, people feel *pain*. With these factors, people do not feel *pain* from absence of these factors, but they also do not feel *pleasure*. These factors include air, health, safety, freedom, and so forth.

"Positive feelings come about when pain abates" (Klein, 2006, p.114). But when *pain* is completely gone, good feelings will also gradually disappear over time, and attention turns to other factors. When freedom is restricted, people experience *pain*. When freedom is restored there is a positive emotional experience. After an individual is released from prison, he or she may feel quite pleasant for days or even weeks. But after a period of time, this factor of freedom is gradually forgotten and the good feelings disappear. Attention turns to other factors. Free people put far less attention on the factor of freedom.

When people's lives or properties are endangered, people experience *pain*. In the process of going from a dangerous state to a safe state, people may experience a positive emotion. If people are in a safe environment for a long time, the factor of safety will no longer influence *pleasure* and *happiness*

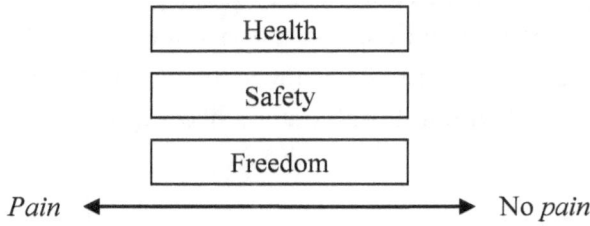

Figure 4.2 Schematic Diagram of *Essential Factors*

The above analyses show that health, freedom and safety can influence *pleasure* during a short period of time. But if people have good health, freedom and safety for long periods of time, then these factors will no longer influence *pleasure* and *happiness* notably. Similarly, when people think that there is inequality, lack of freedom and democracy in the society they live, or being treated unfairly, they feel *pain*. But when people live in a free and democratic society for long periods of time, and they do not feel inequality or injustice, these factors will no longer influence *pleasure* and *happiness*. From view of years or decades, these factors are *Essential Factors*.

2. *Pleasure Factors*

The term ***Pleasure Factors*** defined in this book refer to the factors that are more related to *pleasure*. With these factors, people feel *pleasure*. Without these factors, people do not feel *pleasure*, but do not feel *pain* from the absence of these factors such as an unexpected bonus, curiosity satisfied and self-actualization.

Sometimes people get an unexpected bonus at work and feel quite happy. People win a lottery prize and feel excited. When traveling, curiosity is satisfied and people feel pleased. If a person's career reaches the stage of self-actualization, he or she can feel comfortable and cheerful for a longer period of time.

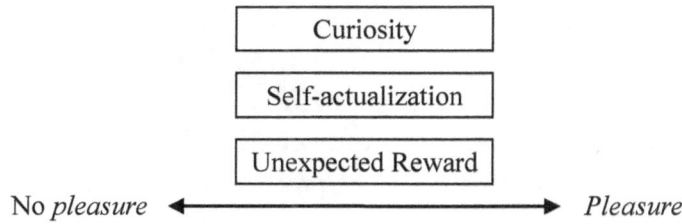

Figure 4.3   Schematic Diagram of *Pleasure Factors*

From view of years or decades, these factors are *Pleasure Factors*. People who frequently have these factors will easily experience *happiness*.

3. *Essential—Pleasure Factors*

The term **Essential—Pleasure Factors** defined in this book refer to the factors that are related to both *pain* and *pleasure*. Without these factors, people feel *pain*. With these factors, people feel *pleasure*. For example: love versus loss of love, kinship versus lack of kinship, respect versus discrimination, and gambling wins versus losses.

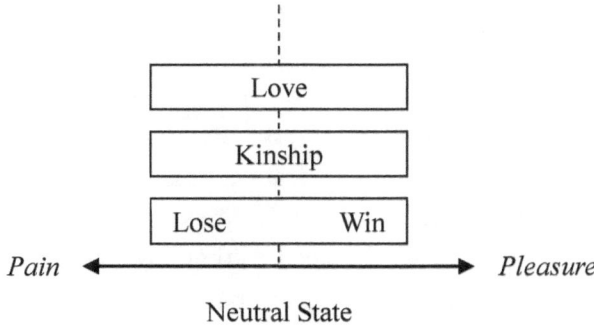

Figure 4.4 Schematic Diagram of *Essential—Pleasure Factors*

People feel *pain* when there is a lack of love in their lives. With love, they feel satisfied. Being passionate in love or being in a honeymoon period, they can be elated. When students are admitted to their top choice of universities, their parents feel very pleased. Conversely, if they fail the entrance exams, their parents are frustrated. People feel happy when family members win big money. People feel sad when a family member suffers from a serious disease. Being discriminated against, being despised, or not being respected by others can make people feel hurt and angry. Being respected, admired by others will make people feel glad. When making money in the stock market, people feel very pleasant, while losing money people feel very sad.

From view of years or decades, these factors are *Essential—Pleasure Factors*. Without these factors for long periods of time, people feel *pain* and misery in their life. With these factors for long periods of time, people more easily experience *happiness*.

Another example of *Essential—Pleasure Factors* is housing. Housing has a variety of functions, two of which are:

(1) Having a basic living space;

(2) As a symbol of social status or success, etc.

Since housing is both a necessity and a luxury, it encompasses both *Essential Factors* and *Pleasure Factors*. Housing with small space that meets basic living requirements is a necessity, and belongs to *Essential Factors*. Homeless people feel *pain*. People with basic housing do not feel *pain* from absence of housing, but also do not feel *pleasure*.

Luxurious housing with large area, in addition to meet the basic living requirements, also functions as a symbol of social status or success. Luxurious housing is a luxury, and belongs to *Pleasure Factors*. The luxury home owners are respected in society and that gives *pleasure*. People without luxury housing, do not feel *pleasure* from it, but may not necessarily feel *pain* from the absence of it either.

These classifications are approximate and may not be accurate, but can be used to analyze the problems and give the necessary conditions for *happiness* described below.

Necessary Conditions for Happiness

Necessary conditions for *happiness* are also the prerequisites for *happiness*. Without these conditions, it is difficult for people to feel *happiness*. Even with the conditions, people may not necessarily feel *happiness*, because the other factors can also cause *pain*. But without these prerequisites, people feel more *pain* and no *happiness* at all. These conditions are prior conditions for achieving *happiness*.

The *Essential-Pleasure Factors* can be divided into two stages.

(1) Elementary stage

Essential—Pleasure Factors exhibit mainly as *Essential Factors* in the elementary stage. For example, in the elementary stage of kinship, people don't feel a lack of kinship, nor do they suffer from lack of kinship. There is no grief originating from family members and relatives going through hard times. In the elementary stage of love, people do not feel *pain* from lack of love, but do not have passion either. In the elementary stage, people who have basic housing don't feel a *need* for shelter; people do not feel being discriminated against, and so forth. In other words, the necessities of life are met. People do not feel *pain* from lack of the necessities of life.

(2) Senior stage

Essential—Pleasure Factors exhibit mainly as *Pleasure Factors* in the senior stage. For example, in the senior stage of kinship, people can obtain *pleasure* from kinship, such as the joy parents feel when their children are admitted to prestigious universities. In the senior stage of love, people are elated, such as being in the passionate love stage and the honeymoon period. In the senior stage, people have luxurious housing conditions; people are respected and esteemed by others, and so forth. In other words, the luxuries of life are met.

Necessary conditions for *happiness* are that all *Essential Factors* are satisfied. All *Essential Factors* contain pure *Essential Factors* and the *Essential Factors* exhibited in the elementary stage of *Essential-Pleasure Factors.*

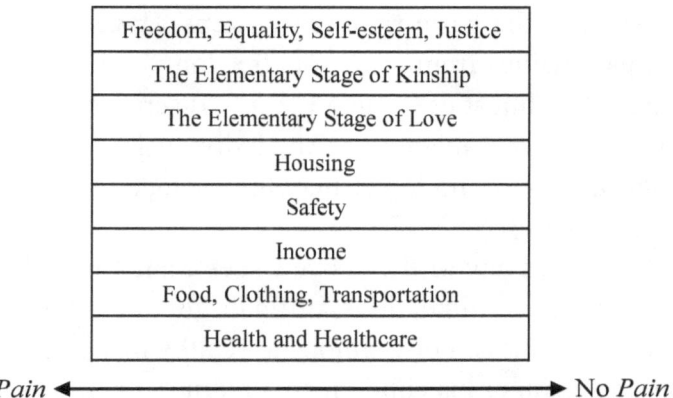

Figure 4.5 Necessary Conditions for *Happiness*

The above analyses suggest the following necessary conditions for *happiness*:

(1) Be physically and mentally healthy and have access to a good healthcare system;

(2) The *Needs* for food, clothing and basic transportation or commuting are met;

(3) The *need* for basic housing is met;

(4) Have reached the elementary stage of love: sexual *needs* are met and feel no *pain* from lack of love, etc;

(5) Have reached the elementary stage of kinship: feel no lack of kinship and no *pain* from lack of kinship, children have access to basic educations, parents are not worried about their children's future, etc;

(6) Have a stable income from work, investments, pensions or unemployment benefits, etc;

(7) Personal and property safety is protected, with good public security, food and medicine safety, etc;

(8) Have the basic rights of citizens. Have no negative feelings arising from lack of freedom and democracy, inequality, injustice, unfairness, discrimination, etc. Self-esteem is satisfied. An individual's situation or circumstances are no lower than the average level of his or her *Similar Reference Group*.

As long as any of the above issues cannot be solved for long periods of time, it is difficult for an individual to achieve *happiness*. For example, a wealthy man has chronic, incurable pain, or his children are on drugs, or he lacks love. If these problems cannot be solved with money, these problems are often the focus of his attention. It becomes difficult to enjoy the *pleasure* from his wealth as the other issues overshadow it. Another example is a married couple deeply in love. They can't enjoy the *pleasure* from love for a long period of time if their basic survival *needs* are not met.

The *Similar Reference Group* is one major factor which has a great impact on an individual's level of *happiness*. For example, at an alumni reunion, people tend to involuntarily calculate the gap between themselves and the other alumni. The reunion can lead to anxiety and worry from evaluations of personal success in career. If a person's situation is always below the average level of his or her alumni for four consecutive years, then he or she is likely to find an excuse not to participate in such an alumni reunion in the fourth year.

A happy individual basically possesses these necessary conditions. These conditions are only necessary conditions for *happiness*, not the sufficient conditions for *happiness*. The necessary condition for *happiness* is that the basic *needs* for survival and reproduction or *Essential Factors* are satisfied for long periods of time.

Only when the necessary conditions for *happiness* are met, is there a neutral platform. It is possible to have more opportunities and more time for individuals to experience *pleasure* and achieve the maximum *happiness* in their lifetime.

Individual Features defined in this book include not only some hereditary factors such as blood type, skin color and personality characteristics, but also some environmental factors such as values, education, abilities and skills. According to the physiological mechanism of *pleasure* in figure 2.2, people can achieve long-term *happiness* relatively easily when their *Individual Features* match or fit into their environments. The viewpoint of "person-environment fit" (Diener, 2009a, p.39) is reasonable to some extent, but not complete. As a step further, this book argues that people can achieve long-term *happiness* relatively easily when they are in situations that match not only their personality characteristics and skills, but also their values. For example, imagine that a handicapped man with the personality characteristics of perseverance, hardworking and ambition spent his whole life in a small Buddhist temple in countryside. He could live a happy life because he needn't work hard for survival. He could live on the money donated to the temple by Buddhists. He thought he would have a bright future in reincarnation or afterlife after he studied and practiced Buddhism hard this life. His ***reference group*** (Hughes, 2002, p.128) was mainly his peers in the temple. Because he studied diligently and practiced hard, his status or circumstance could be higher than the average level of his peers in the temple. In other words, his values, personalities and skills matched the environment in which he lived. Imagine another situation that the handicapped man spent his whole life in a cosmopolitan city where life's competition was fierce. He wished to make a large sum of money, but he would not be able to because he was handicapped and did not have good skills. Despite his great efforts to study diligently and work hard, his status or circumstance would still be at the bottom of the society. His *reference group* was mainly the individuals around him in the city. He would probably live a miserable life at the bottom of his *reference group* because his values, personalities and skills did not match the environment in which he lived.

In the short term, sufficient conditions for *pleasure* can exist. For example, people can feel *pleasure* when eating after being hungry for two days. In the long term, there is no a universal path to *happiness* applicable to everyone. There are always some people in society who achieve far less *happiness* than others in their lifetime because of the *Relativity* of *Pleasure Intensity*.

Chapter 5

Measuring Pleasure

This chapter presents the principles and methods of quantitative measurement of *pleasure* within a short period of time. Human brain cannot subjectively perceive the accurate numerical value of the level of *pleasure*, just as human ear can not perceive the accurate numerical value of the strength of sound. Human ear can perceive one sound being louder than another, but it cannot accurately determine how much louder it is. However, under certain conditions, by establishing the causality between a sound source and an auditory sense, it is possible to accurately determine how much one sound is louder than another by means of measuring the intensities of the two sound sources using scientific methods. Another example is that one can perceives his or her heart beating faster when running fast than when lying in bed, but one can't determine the quantitative difference between the two situations. However, electrocardiogram instruments can accurately measure the quantitative differences in heart rate.

The principles and methods presented in this chapter are to set up the causality between a certain factor (the cause) and the *pleasure* (the consequence) produced by the factor only. Then the level of the subjectively experienced *pleasure* can be measured quantitatively using scientific methods.

Mathematical Definitions

Some functions defined in this chapter are used for measuring the intensity of *need* and *pleasure* in scientific experiments and questionnaires.

1. *Need Intensity N* is defined as follows:

$N = N(t)$, which is a function of time t.

$N(t)$ is a psychological magnitude representing an individual's subjective experience. At any moment t, the level of subjective *need* is positively related to $N(t)$, where $N(t)$ describes the level of an individual's need for external stimulus at the moment.

$N > 0$ means that there are *needs*, $N = 0$ means that there is no *need*.

There is no *need* at the *ground state* $B_0(t)$, then $N = 0$.

N_i is defined as **Need Intensity** of the i-th stimulus to an individual, where i = 1, 2, 3,......, stands for different *needs* of an individual.

Let N_1 be the *Need Intensity* of food. For example, an individual does not want to eat any more right after he had a meal, then $N_1 = 0$. Suppose one did not have any food during the past 48 hours, one's N_1 must have increased with the rising of one's hungry level. Therefore N_1 may be different at different moments, e.g. at 8, 24, 48 hours after he or she had a full meal.

The unit of *Need Intensity* is NIU (*Need Intensity* Unit). For example, the unit of food-related *Need Intensity* can be defined as follows:

The food-related *Need Intensity* equals 1 FNIU (Food-related *Need Intensity* Unit) when blood glucose = 3.8mmol/L. The other experimental parameters can be defined similarly.

2. *Pleasure Intensity P* is defined in Chapter 3.

$P = P(t)$, which is a function of time t.

$P(t)$ is a psychological magnitude representing an individual's subjective experience. At any moment t, the level of subjective *pleasure* is positively related to $P(t)$, where $P(t)$ describes the strength for an individual to experience *pleasure* at the moment .

$P > 0$ stands for *pleasure*, $P < 0$ stands for *pain*, $P = 0$ stands for neither *pleasure* nor *pain*.

There is no *pleasure* and no *pain* at the *ground state* $B_0(t)$, then $P = 0$.

A deficiency in such definition is that $P(t)$ includes indiscriminately all kinds of positive emotional experiences. In fact, different positive emotional experiences originate from different sources. For example, *pleasure* arising from satisfying appetite is different from *pleasure* of sexual intercourse. The two cannot replace each other. The physiological basis of these two kinds of *pleasures* may also be different. This book describes approximately all kinds of positive emotional experiences with P. This may be a simplification from otherwise more rigorous and comprehensive descriptions of P. Such simplification is to facilitate the analysis of the problem, to focus on the main factors, to draw the features of *Pleasure Intensity*.

The unit of *Pleasure Intensity* is PIU (*Pleasure Intensity Unit*). For example, the unit of the food-related *Pleasure Intensity P₁* can be defined as follows:

Excluding other factors, in the ERP waveforms, the food-related *Pleasure Intensity P₁* is 1 FPIU (Food-related *Pleasure Intensity* Unit) when the average voltage in a time window from 150-1000ms equals 1 microvolt. The other experimental parameters can be defined similarly.

3. Amount of *pleasure p*

p is defined as the amount of *pleasure* which describes how much *pleasure* within tens of seconds, days or months.

p_i is the amount of *pleasure* evoked by the i-th event, which is an integral calculated from:

$$p_i = \int_{T1}^{T2} P_i(t)dt,$$

where T_1 is the initial time of the i-th event, T_2 is the ending time of the i-th event, $P_i(t)$ is the *Pleasure Intensity* of the i-th event at the moment *t*.

For example, having a dinner, watching a tennis game, and attending a concert are all events.

Let the average *Pleasure Intensity* of the i-th event be $\bar{P}_i$, then $p_i = \bar{P}_i \times (T_2 - T_1)$.

$p_i > 0$ stands for *pleasure*, $p_i < 0$ stands for *pain*.

The unit of *p* is PU (Pleasure Unit).

1 PU can be defined as 1 PIU (*Pleasure Intensity* Unit) multiplied by the unit time, that is

1 PU = 1 PIU × 1 second.

How is the amount of *pleasure* for an event calculated?

For example, a person spends half an hour for lunch.

Without considering other factors, suppose that the average amplitude of the food-related ERP component is 1 microvolt measured in EEG in the eating process, corresponding to the average *Pleasure Intensity* = 1 PIU , then the amount of *pleasure* during this period (1800 seconds) equals 1800×1=1800 PU.

It is important to note that the subjective emotional experiences during this period for lunch depend not only on the quality of the food that is an external stimulus, but also on the *brain physiological state* which is related to the other external stimuli and the physical brain, as well as states of consciousness. If a person remembers a past painful experience while eating, the person may feel sad. If a person thinks boring things from work while eating, the person may feel upset. If a person watches funny story from TV while eating, the person may feel pleasant. Therefore, the person's attention should be only focused on food during the period for lunch.

Similarly, if a person works for four hours in the afternoon, the subjective emotional experiences in the afternoon depend not only on the content of work, but also on various other external stimuli, the physical brain and states of consciousness. In other words, the amount of *pleasure* within a day is related not only to the events and the environments on the day, but also to past events, and events are expected to happen in the future, and so forth.

How is the amount of *pleasure* within a day calculated? One method is that all activities within a day are divided into different events. There is only one thing in each event. For example, if there are two things in the content of work in the morning. One is a meeting and the other is to go out to meet a customer. Then the work in the morning can be divided into two events. Suppose that activities within a day are composed of the following events:

The first event: "Maintenance Activities" from waking up to breakfast, the amount of *pleasure* is p_1;

The second event: having breakfast, the amount of *pleasure* during this period is p_2;

The third event: working in the morning, the amount of *pleasure* is p_3;

The fourth event: having lunch, the amount of *pleasure* is p_4;

The fifth event: working in the afternoon, the amount of *pleasure* is p_5;

The sixth event: having dinner, the amount of *pleasure* is p_6;

The seventh event: "Leisure Activities" after dinner till going to bed, the amount of *pleasure* is p_7.

The total amount of *pleasure* within the day p(day) is described as follows:

$$p \text{ (day)} = p_1 + p_2 + p_3 + p_4 + p_5 + p_6 + p_7 = \sum_{i=1}^{7} p_i$$

p (day) > 0 stands for more *pleasures* than *pains*.
p (day) < 0 stands for more *pains* than *pleasures*.

Similarly, let the total amount of *pleasure* within a month be p(month), then

$$p(\text{month}) \ = \ \sum p(\text{day}),\ \text{summing the amount of}$$

pleasure for every day in the month.

Experimental Principles and Methods

1. Measuring partial derivatives (Kaplan, 2004, p.83) of the *brain physiological state B.*

The *brain physiological state B* at any moment in time is determined by the interaction of all external stimuli and internal physiological factors, as well as the state of consciousness at the moment. The integrated result of all factors influences the *brain physiological state*. For example, a person with stomachache is having dinner with friends. While eating and talking, the person is informed about his or her winning a lottery prize, at the same time he or she feels a little pain in the stomach. The EEG recordings at this time are an integrated result of the stomachache, the food stimulus, and the informational stimulus, as well as what his or her attention is focused on. Researchers cannot distinguish which amplitude and latency of EEG waveforms are caused by the stomachache, the food or by the news of winning a lottery.

That is, B is a function of the variables K_1, K_2, ... K_i, ..., C_1, C_2, ... C_i, ..., S_1, S_2, ... S_i, ...

$$B = B(K_1, K_2, ... K_i, ..., C_1, C_2, ... C_i, ..., S_1, S_2, ... S_i, ...)$$

where, K_1, K_2, ... K_i, ... are physiological factors of the body, such as stomachache, trauma, liver disease, lung infection, etc.

C_1, C_2, ... C_i ,... are states of consciousness, such as thinking about problems, remembering something that happened in the past, making a cognitive evaluation of the quality of life during a period of time, etc.

S_1, S_2, ... S_i, ... are external stimuli, such as light, sound, food and lottery prize news, etc.

Because many variables are not completely independent of each other, changes in one variable may cause changes in another. For example, external temperature rising too high (a change in an external stimulus) can cause the skin to be burned (a change in a physiological factor of the body).

In other words, changes in B are often the result of changes in multiple independent variables. An infinitesimal amount of change in B is a total differential (Kaplan, 2004, p.86) of B, that is,

$$dB = (\partial B/\partial K_1)dK_1 + (\partial B/\partial K_2)dK_2, ..., (\partial B/\partial K_i)dK_i, ...,$$
$$+ (\partial B/\partial C_1)dC_1 + (\partial B/\partial C_2)dC_2, ..., (\partial B/\partial C_i)dC_i, ...,$$
$$+ (\partial B/\partial S_1)dS_1 + (\partial B/\partial S_2)dS_2, ..., (\partial B/\partial S_i)dS_i, ...$$

where, $(\partial B/\partial K_1)$ is the partial derivative of B with respect to K_1, $(\partial B/\partial K_2)$ is the partial derivative of B with respect to K_2, ..., $(\partial B/\partial K_i)$ is the partial derivative of B with respect to K_i.

Similarly, $(\partial B/\partial C_1)$ the partial derivative of B with respect to C_1, $(\partial B/\partial C_2)$ the partial derivative of B with respect to C_2,..., $(\partial B/\partial C_i)$ the partial derivative of B with respect to C_i.

$(\partial B/\partial S_1)$ the partial derivative of B with respect to S_1, $(\partial B/\partial S_2)$ the partial derivative of B with respect to S_2, ..., $(\partial B/\partial S_i)$ the partial derivative of B with respect to S_i.

(Assume that B has continuous first partial derivatives).

In order to measure the partial derivative of $B(t)$ with respect to a variable during experiments, the following should be noted:

(1) One variable alone changes with the other variables fixed

For example, let S_2 be an external physical stimulus—light. To measure $(\partial B/\partial S_2)$—changes in B caused only by light, researchers must design an experimental condition that only the external light changes while the other variables remain unchanged. In the experiments, keep:

$dK_1 = 0$, $dK_2 = 0$, ..., $dK_i = 0$,.... There are no pains in the body. There are no such body's factors that the respondent's attention is focused on.

$dC_1 = 0$, $dC_3 = 0$, ..., $dC_i = 0$,.... The respondent's attention is focused on the light only, without thinking of the events about work or family that have nothing to do with the experiment.

$dS_1 = 0$, $dS_3 = 0$, ..., $dS_i = 0$,.... In addition to light, there are no changes in other external stimuli.

Under such conditions, the changes measured in B are approximately caused by the changes in light alone.

(2) Fully take advantage of selective attention

Researchers should make the respondents focus on the stimulus that is designed to be measured as an independent variable in the experiments, and pay no attention to other factors. Because attention is focused on an event, changes in this event make the maximum contributions to $B(t)$, changes in the other factors are ruled out or ignored by the brain. Therefore, experimental environments should facilitate the respondents to focus their attention on the independent variable being tested in the experiments. The respondents should be actively cooperative with researchers to maximize the effects of selective attention.

(3) Researchers should conduct a sufficient number of experiments, such as 10 or more times for the same person, during as short a period of time as possible (such as a few weeks). Changes in dK_1, dK_2, ..., dK_i are assumed to be negligible in the short term. The multiple measuring results should be averaged. Strictly speaking, at different times of experiments, dK_1, dK_2 ,..., dK_i are not equal to zero theoretically, because the physiological factors of the body are always changing. Therefore, the interval of conducting experiments for the same person should not be too long, otherwise the physiological factors of the body may change so greatly that changes in dK_1, dK_2 , ..., dK_i can not be ignored.

Researchers cannot use methods of the *experimental group* comparing with the *control group* (Hughs, 2002, p.26) in normal psychological experiments and surveys. Because $dK_1 \neq 0$, $dK_2 \neq 0$, ..., $d K_i \neq 0$,... for different respondents.

B(t) can be measured using instruments and equipment. *P(t)* cannot be directly measured with experimental methods, but can be obtained by questionnaires.

At the same time of measuring *B(t)*, researchers should ask the respondents to answer questionnaires, to make the measured *B(t)* and *P(t)* synchronized in time. Only in this way, may researchers find the correlates between the brain physiological quantity *B(t)* and the brain psychological magnitude *P(t)*, and summarize the corresponding relationship between *P*(t) and some elements of the *brain physiological state B(t)*, based on the experimental results and questionnaires.

2. Measuring elements of $B(t)$

Changes in different elements of $B(t)$ can be measured using different techniques. For example, "positron emission tomography (PET) scans for glucose use in the brain" (Solso, 2005, p.53).

Functional magnetic resonance imaging (fMRI) detects increased blood flow to activated areas of the brain, thus displaying function and structure (Solso, 2005, p.56).

Magnetic resonance imaging (MRI) scans provide still images of structures of the brain (Solso, 2005, p.55).

Mental Activity Network Scanner (MANSCAN), which can record as many as 250 images of cerebral activity per second (Solso, 2005, p.52).

A computed axial tomograghy (CT) scan also provides a still image that shows the structure of the brain (Solso, 2005, p. 53).

An even more sophisticated version of the CT technique, the dynamic spatial reconstructor (DSR), shows internal structures in three dimensions (Solso, 2005, p.53).

Magnetoencephalography (MEG) uses a machine that measures brain activity from the outside of the head by detecting the faint magnetic fields that the brain activity produces. MEG produces an "activity map" or "functional images" of the brain (Solso, 2005, p.56).

Blood pressure, heart rate and electrodermal activity can be measured by polygraph.

All above quantities that can be measured are elements of $B(t)$.

3. Measuring ERP

The experimental method is illustrated with ERP (event-related potential) as an example below.

EEGs can show us how long it takes the brain to process stimuli (Solso, 2005, p.52). "Definition of the term ERP component is: Scalp-recorded neural activity that is generated in a given neuroanatomical module when a specific computational operation is performed" (Luck, 2005, p.59). For example, the N400 is a language-related ERP component, the LRP is a motor-related ERP component (Luck, 2005, p.94).

In EEG, amplitude and latency of an ERP component can be as two elements of the *brain physiological state B*. Changes in the amplitude of an ERP component evoked by a stimulus can be measured with the other elements of *B* fixed. The changes can be considered as the only cause arising from the stimulus in the measurement periods of time. The amount of changes in amplitude, for example, can be considered as the partial derivative of amplitude with respect to the stimulus.

Thus, it is possible to establish relationships between amplitude of ERP component and *Pleasure Intensity* by recording EEG of a respondent and asking the respondent to answer questionnaires simultaneously. Quantitative evaluations can possibly be made for *Pleasure Intensity* according to the amplitude of ERP component.

Assume the food-related ERP component exists. Conducting a sufficient number of experiments for the same respondent, researchers may find out the food-related ERP component for this respondent. Similarly, conducting a sufficient number of experiments for many respondents, researchers may find out the food-related ERP component for each respondent. However, hereditary factors and environmental factors differ between individuals. The food-related ERP components generally differ between individuals. How are the food-related ERP components compared between individuals? ERP *Difference Waves* (Luck, 2005, p.63) and ERP *Amplitude Normalization* (Urbach, 2006, p.333) can be used to compare the food-related ERP components between individuals.

Let the average amplitude of the food-related ERP waveforms be A_m, and the average amplitude of *ground state* at the same position be A_0, then the *Difference Waves* $= (A_m - A_0)$, the *Normalized Amplitude* $= A_m/A_0$. *Normalized Difference Waves* is defined as $(A_m - A_0)/A_0$. Then,

(1) $(A_m - A_0)$ can be compared between individuals;

(2) (A_m/A_0) can be compared between individuals;

(3) $(A_m - A_0)/A_0$ can be compared between individuals.

Similarly, latency of the food-related ERP can be analyzed in the same way.

Difference Waves and *Amplitude Normalization* methods of ERP components remove or substantially reduce the effects arising from individuals' hereditary factors and environmental factors. The relative $(A_m - A_0)$, A_m/A_0 and $(A_m - A_0)/A_0$ can be obtained. In this way, it is possible to compare the relative food-related ERP components between individuals and to summarize the universal regularity for the majority of people. This is like that everyone is different, but electrocardiograms of most people are similar.

During the experiment, it is impossible for other variables to remain unchanged absolutely. That is the problem of experimental errors which are beyond the scope of this book.

Hypothetical Experiments

Assume there is a *pleasure* when an appetite is satisfied, and there exists a food-related ERP component in EEG, its amplitude, latency, and any other parameters can be measured. Let the food-related *Pleasure Intensity* be P_l and the averaged amplitude of the food-related ERP component be A_m. The purpose of this experiment is to construct the relationship between A_m and P_l.

1. Experimental Design

Let S_1 be the food factor (external food stimulus), C_1 the state of consciousness with attention being focused on food.

Researchers should change the food variable alone with all other variables fixed. Researchers should carefully select respondents for the experiments. Physical examination on respondents should be conducted in order to ensure that respondents are in good health without illnesses. All physiological indicators of respondents should be healthy. During the experiment, no any sudden pains or discomforts occur in the body such as a stomachache. That is, researchers should keep physiological factors of the body unchanged, so as to ensure $dK_1 = 0$, $dK_2 = 0$, ..., $dK_i = 0$,....

In addition, respondents' work should be in normal state, without worrying about being laid off, etc. The respondents should have a normal interpersonal relationship in their work units. Also, the respondents should be in normal relationships with their spouses and family members, free of extreme situations of honeymoon period or lovelorn period. All aspects of the respondents' family members such as parents, brothers, sisters, children should be in normal state too. In the process of experiments, the respondents only focus their attention on food, they cannot be possibly distracted by the things about their work, family, children, and so forth, so as to ensure that $dC_2 = 0$, $dC_3 = 0$, ..., $dC_i = 0$,....

During the experiments, food is only one external stimulus, there are no changes in other external stimuli, so as to ensure that $dS_2 = 0$, $dS_3 = 0$, ..., $dS_i = 0$,....

In order to make the impacts of other factors on the respondents be negligible, researchers should design experimental conditions and situations to make the respondents only focus on food. For example, before experiments, the respondents are asked to fast enough long time, such as 36 hours, 48 hours, or more, so that respondents are in a starving state. During the experiments, respondents are too hungry to think of the other things about work, family, daily life and so forth, except for food (respondents are in the C_1 state).

Researchers continuously record the respondents' EEG while they are eating food. Owing to selective attention, changes in EEG during this period can be considered to be caused only by food. That is, the EEG recordings during this period are approximately the EEG corresponding to the food-related *Pleasure Intensity* of the respondents. The amount of changes in amplitude can be approximately considered as the partial derivative of amplitude with respect to food:

$$(\partial A_m / \partial S_1) \approx \triangle A_m / \triangle S_1$$

where $\triangle S_1$ stands for the changes in food stimulus (after and before eating).

2. Experimental Procedures

(1) Measurements taken exactly at the same time

Take one respondent as example below. Researchers should write down the starting time of eating, record continuously the ERP components of EEG in the process of eating, meanwhile, ask the respondent to answer the *pleasure* questionnaire every two minutes (write down exact moments in time for each answer):

the worst taste   the best taste
(the most *pain*)   (the most *pleasure*)
    -5, -4, -3, -2, -1 , 0 , 1, 2, 3, 4, 5

After the experiment, researchers compare the amplitude of ERP component with the numerical scale answered by the respondent at the same moment in time, and then try to establish a relationship between the ERP amplitude and the numerical scale of *Pleasure Intensity* in terms of a time-sequence.

(2) Average amplitude

Suppose it will take 30 minutes to finish eating.

Immediately after eating, researchers ask the respondent to answer the average *Pleasure Intensity* within the 30 minutes of eating $\bar{P}_1$:

the worst taste   the best taste
(the most *pain*)   (the most *pleasure*)
-5, -4, -3, -2, -1 , 0 , 1, 2, 3, 4, 5

It should be noted that the answer should be the respondents' subjective emotional experience in the process of eating, not the overall cognitive evaluation on the food.

After the experiment, researchers average the ERP amplitude over 30 minutes, and compare the averaged amplitude with the numerical scale $\bar{P}_1$ answered by the respondent and then try to set up a relationship between the averaged ERP amplitude and the averaged numerical scale of *Pleasure Intensity*. Researchers can also analyze the correlates between the latency of the ERP component and the numerical scale of the food-related *Pleasure Intensity* after the experiment.

If researchers conduct a sufficient number of experiments for the same respondent, and find out the same waveforms in these experiments, then the waveforms are the food-related ERP component for this respondent. Researchers can compare the amplitude of the food-related ERP component (physiological quantity) with the numerical scale $\bar{P}_1$ of *Pleasure Intensity* (psychological magnitude), and summarize the relationship between the waveforms of the food-related ERP component and the food-related *Pleasure Intensity* at the same moment for the respondent.

If permitted by the experimental conditions, researchers can continuously record the level of blood glucose, cardiac index, skin electrical activity, etc. as indicators in the process of eating, then try to find the correlates among the food-related *Pleasure Intensity P_1* and the level of blood glucose, cardiac index, skin electrical activity indicators, etc. These correlates can be as reference indicators to set up the relationship between the amplitude of the food-related ERP component and the food-related *Pleasure Intensity P_1*.

3. Hypothesized Experimental Results

Assume that there exists a food-related ERP component. The averaged amplitude of the food-related ERP component A_m positively correlates to the food-related *Pleasure Intensity P_1*.

4. Other Experiments

Let N_1 be the food-related *Need Intensity*; P_2 the water-related *Pleasure Intensity*; P_3 the sexual-intercourse-related *Pleasure Intensity*; P_4 the win-money-related *Pleasure Intensity* in gambling; P_5 the cognition-related *Pleasure Intensity*; P_6 the meditation-related *Pleasure Intensity*; P_7 the drugs-related *Pleasure Intensity*.

Similar experiments from the above illustrations can be conducted to see if there exist any relationships between amplitude of the food-related *need* ERP component and the food-related *Need Intensity N_1*; between amplitude of the water-related ERP component and the water-related *Pleasure Intensity P_2*; between amplitude of the sexual-intercourse- related ERP component and the sexual-intercourse-related *Pleasure Intensity* P_3; between amplitude of the win- money-related ERP component and the win-money-related *Pleasure Intensity* P_4; between amplitude of the cognition- related ERP component and the cognition-related *Pleasure Intensity* P_5; between amplitude of the meditation-related ERP component and the meditation-related *Pleasure Intensity* P_6; and between amplitude of the drugs-related ERP component and the drugs-related *Pleasure Intensity* P_7.

Hypothesized experimental results are as follows:

(1) The level of blood glucose negatively correlates to the food-related *Need Intensity*. The lower the level of blood glucose, the stronger the food-related *Need Intensity* N_1 is.

(2)There exists a food-related *need* ERP component. With the increase of degree of hunger, the amplitude of the food-related *need* ERP component positively correlates to the food-related *need Intensity* N_1.

(3) There exists a water-related ERP component. The amplitude of the water-related ERP component positively correlates to the water-related *Pleasure Intensity* P_2.

(4) There exists a sexual-intercourse-related ERP component. The amplitude of the sexual-intercourse-related ERP component positively correlates to the sexual-intercourse-related *Pleasure Intensity* P_3.

(5) There exists a win-money-related ERP component. The amplitude of the win-money-related ERP component positively correlates to the win-money-related *Pleasure Intensity* P_4. There also exists a lose-money-related ERP component. The amplitude of the lose-money-related ERP component positively correlates to the lose-money-related

Pain Intensity (minus *Pleasure Intensity*). The differences between the lose-money-related ERP component and the win-money-related ERP component might not just be the sign differences.

(6) There exists a cognition-related ERP component. The amplitude of the cognition-related ERP component positively correlates to the cognition-related *Pleasure Intensity P_5*.

(7) There exists a meditation-related ERP component. The amplitude of the meditation-related ERP component positively correlates to the meditation-related *Pleasure Intensity P_6*.

(8) There exists a drugs-related ERP component. The amplitude of the drugs-related ERP component positively correlates to the drugs-related *Pleasure Intensity P_7*.

The above experiments can be conducted by using other techniques such as MEG, fMRI, MANSCAN, PET mentioned previously.

Chapter 6

Measuring Happiness

Mathematical Definitions

The amount of *happiness* is expressed as $\mathcal{H}$ which describes how much *happiness* within years or decades.

According to the definition of *happiness* in Chapter 1, $\mathcal{H}$ is equal to the sum of many small *pleasures*.

The mathematical relationship between $\mathcal{H}$ and p is:

$\mathcal{H} = \sum p$ (day), summing the amount of *pleasure* for every day during a longer period of time.

Let the total amount of *happiness* within one year be $\mathcal{H}$(year), then

$\mathcal{H}$ (year) $= \sum p$(month), summing the amount of *pleasure* for every month in the year.

Let the total amount of *happiness* for a person in his or her entire life be $\mathcal{H}$(M), then

$\mathcal{H}$ (M) $= \sum \mathcal{H}$ (year) $= \sum p$(month) $= \sum p$(day),

summing the amount of *pleasure* for every day in his or her lifetime, where M is the number of days of his or her lifetime.

$\mathcal{H}$ (M) represents the amount of *happiness* during the period from one's birth to the end of life.

$\mathcal{H}$ (M) >> 0 stands for a person who was very happy in his or her lifetime. $\mathcal{H}$ (M) << 0 stands for a person who was very unhappy in his or her lifetime.

$\mathcal{H}$ (M) $\sim$ 0 stands for a person whose life was equally happy and unhappy in his or her lifetime. The amount of *pleasure* was almost the same as that of *pain*.

Let the total amount of *happiness* for a person who has attended college for four years be $\mathcal{H}$ (four years), then:

$$\mathcal{H} \text{ (four years)} = \sum p(\text{month}) = \sum p(\text{day}),$$ summing

the amount of *pleasure* for every day or every month during the four years.

Let the total amount of *happiness* for a person from his or her birth to the present be $\mathcal{H}$(D), then

$$\mathcal{H}(D) = \sum p(\text{day}),$$ summing the amount of *pleasure* for

every day from his or her birth to the present, where D is the number of days from his or her birth to the present.

Scientific Methods

A hypothetical scientific method of quantitatively measuring the total amount of *happiness* for one year is illustrated with ERP components in EEG as an example below, assuming that researchers had obtained EEG waveforms of the food-related ERP component, the water-related ERP component, and other components for a respondent under certain conditions in a laboratory using experimental methods illustrated in Chapter 5.

Assume that researchers developed a tiny EEG instrument. This EEG instrument could be placed in a certain position on a respondent's body. It would not have any effect on the respondent's daily life, and could record the respondent's EEGs anytime and anywhere. The EEG waveforms could be sent by radio signals to the researchers' computers. Researchers could compare the respondent's EEG waveforms with the EEG waveforms of the food-related ERP component, the water-related ERP component and other components obtained previously in the laboratory, analyze and calculate the amount of *pleasure* each day respectively.

With the development of science and technology, let's assume that researchers could develop a tiny multi-functional instrument. This instrument could be placed on a certain position of a respondent's body. It would not have any effect on the respondent's daily life, and could continuously record the respondent's parameters of the *brain physiological state* such as EEGs, the level of blood glucose, amount of dopamine, amount of morphine and so forth for 365 days. All these parameters could be sent by radio signals to the researchers' computers. Researchers could figure out the total amount of *happiness* within one year by adding the amounts of *pleasure* within 365 days.

Analyses of Happiness Scales

The previous hypotheses indicate that researchers could theoretically record a respondent's EEGs or parameters of the *brain physiological state* for a long period of time using instruments, and then figure out the amount of the respondent's *happiness*. However, it is very difficult to make it really happen with the current technology. The experimental instruments require a high degree of precision.

Under present experimental conditions, researchers can only estimate a respondent's level of *happiness* during a long period of time by using questionnaires. Because respondents' judgments can be influenced by memory biases (Diener, 2009b, p.162) and transient factors at the time of completing the scale , and because some respondents may not necessarily answer questions honestly, thus the method of questionnaires is only an approximate measurement of *happiness*.

There are a number of scales designed to measure SWB (Diener, 2009a, pp.12-24). Only the widely used Diener's Satisfaction With Life Scale (SWLS) is analyzed in this chapter. Below are five items of the SWLS (Diener, 2009b, p.114).

(1) In most ways my life is close to my ideal.

(2) The conditions of my life are excellent.

(3) I am satisfied with my life.

(4) So far I have gotten the important things I want in life.

(5) If I could live my life over, I would change almost

nothing.

The time frame of the SWLS items is not clear. In daily life, when people talk about happiness, two kinds of time frames are normally related to happiness. One is the overall cognitive evaluation of satisfaction with the current life made at a moment in time, or within a shorter period of time such as a few minutes when people answer the questions on the happiness scales. The other is the aggregation of the emotional experiences of *pleasure* during a longer period of time. The results of assessing happiness in terms of the two different time frames may differ totally.

Whether the term "my life" in the SWLS items (1), (2), (3) refers to the current life (at a moment in time, or at the time of completing the scale) or a process of the life during a past period of time is not clear. People can be very dissatisfied with their current life, but they can be very satisfied with the life during the past year. The current life (at a moment in time) differs totally from a process of the life (during a period of time). The term "life" in items (4) and (5) refers to a process of the life during a period of time, not at a moment in time. There are at least three possible results from the overall evaluation of life satisfaction at the time when a respondent responses to the SWLS.

(1) For the first three items, the respondent's answers refer to the evaluation of the current life (at a moment in time). For the latter two items, the respondent's answers refer to the overall evaluation of the whole past life (during a period of time).

(2) For all five items, the respondent's answers refer to the overall evaluation of the whole past life (during a period

of time).

(3) For all five items, the respondent's answers refer to the aggregation of the emotional experiences of *pleasure* across time (during a period of time from his or her birth to the present).

As above, the methods of response (2) and (3) are different. The results of (2) are influenced by the respondent's values and transit factors at the time of completing the SWLS.

As can be seen from the above analyses, because the time frame of the SWLS is not clear, different respondents may be answering different questions, leading to confused or even contradictory results. Therefore, the authenticity of this type of survey data from the SWLS should not be fully trusted.

The Weighted Scales and the Well-Being Index

According to the above analyses, the term **well-being** defined in this book encompasses both cognitive evaluations of satisfaction at a moment in time and a process of emotional experiences during a period of time. The **Weighted Scales** of *well-being* are designed to contain two parts, the level of satisfaction at a moment in time and the level of *happiness* during a period of time. In addition, in order to more accurately and reasonably estimate a person's *happiness*, and determine which factors are the main factors that influence a person's *happiness*, the *Weighted Scales* also include the following factors.

(1) Weights of factors that influence *happiness*.

In a lifetime, there are many factors influencing a person's *happiness*. The degrees of influence from different factors on a person's *happiness* differ. In other words, the weights of different factors for the same person are different. For example, love and friendship are factors influencing a person's *happiness*, but the degree of influence from love is different from that of influence from friendship.

(2)For different individuals, various factors influencing their *happiness* have different weights. For example, some individuals think income is the most important, but others may think love or family is the most important, depending on different individuals' values.

(3)For the same person, in different stages of life, the weight of the same factor influencing *happiness* will change. For example, young people in general when seeking a mate care more about love. Elderly people with illnesses may be more concerned about health.

(4)Generally speaking, the more a person lacks a certain factor, the greater the factor's weight to him or her is. For example, incomes of young people in good health working only for few years are relatively low. Therefore, the weight of the income factor is relatively large to them, and the weight of the health factor is relatively small. For elderly people suffering from diseases, even though their incomes are much more than young people's incomes, the weights of the health and healthcare factors are relatively large, while the weight of the income factor is relatively small.

There are many factors influencing a person's *happiness*. The degrees of various factors influencing *happiness* can differ substantially between individuals. If scales are designed to include various factors, the scales will be very complicated. As a result, it is very difficult to use them in practice. Therefore, only factors that are regarded as major ones for most people can be put into scales. Some individuals' factors without representative can be put into "other factors" in the scales. Respondents can be asked to specify what other specific factors influencing their *happiness* are relatively large. The *Weighted Scales* are presented in detail below based on the above analyses.

1. *The level of satisfaction* S is defined as the overall evaluations of satisfaction with life at a moment in time (at the moment of completing the scale, for example).

$$S = \sum_{i=1} a_i X_i \qquad (6.1)$$

where X_i is a significant factor influencing *the level of satisfaction*, a_i is the weight of this factor. a_i also stands for the degree to which individuals care about this factor, reflecting individuals' preference, where

$$\sum_{i=1} a_i = 100\%$$

Researchers should conduct the survey in two steps. First, respondents can be asked to estimate the weights of various factors influencing *the level of satisfaction* (see Table of Weights of Satisfaction Factors). Second, respondents can be asked to evaluate the contribution of each factor to *the level of satisfaction* respectively (see Table of Evaluation of Satisfaction Level).

(1)Table of Weights of Satisfaction Factors (WSF)

The WSF Table shows the weights of various factors influencing *the level of satisfaction* with the current life. Because it is difficult for a respondent to accurately estimate the weight of a factor, but it is relatively easy for a respondent to rank the priority order of various factors influencing *the level of satisfaction* with the current life. Therefore, it is more practicable for researchers to ask respondents to rank the order of various factors in the WSF Table on a scale from 0 (*no influence*) to 10 (*most influence*) according to the relative degrees of influence from these factors. For each item, select a number from 0 to 10, and fill the number in the WSF Table. A_i in the WSF Table is the number of ordering. The numbers for different factors can be the same.

10 = influence the most

1 = influence the least

0 = no influence

The weight a_i corresponding to the i-th factor can be transformed via A_i.

$$a_i = A_i / \sum_{i=1} A_i \qquad (6.2)$$

Table 6.1 Weights of Satisfaction Factors

Weights (select numbers according to the degrees of influence)	10	9	8	7	6	5	4	3	2	1	0
A_1: Health											
A_2: Job or income											
A_3: Love or marriage											
A_4: Education											
A_5 : Housing and environment											
A_6: Social safety											
A_7: Transportation system											
A_8: Kinship or family											
A_9: Social status											
A_{10} : Basic rights											
A_{11}: Others											
A_{12}:											

Instructions:

A_1: Health (including the condition of receiving medical treatment)

A_2: Job or income (including investments, pensions, unemployment benefits, etc.)

A_3: Love or marriage (whether there is a lack of love or a lack of affection with partner)

A_4: Education (including their own and their children's educational conditions)

A_5: Housing and environment (including air quality, environment health, public facilities and services such as libraries, parks, and fitness centers)

A_6: Social safety (including personal and property safety, food and medicine safety, public security, etc.)

A_7: Transportation system (including commuting and traveling outside of the place of residence)

A_8: Kinship or family (including the living conditions of children, parents, brothers and sisters)

A_9: Social status (the relative position in the *Similar Reference Group*, including interpersonal relationships)

A_{10}: Basic rights (including freedom, democracy, equality, fairness, justice, respect from others, faith, and the quality of governmental services)

A_{11} and A_{12}: Other factors (ask respondents to specify what other factors that also influence their satisfaction with the current life. Examples can be natural disasters such as earthquakes and typhoons or anything else not previously covered)

(2)Table of Evaluation of Satisfaction Level (ESL)

The ESL Table shows respondent's evaluations of *the level of satisfaction* with the current life. Respondents can be asked to evaluate the contribution of each factor to their satisfaction with the current life respectively. For each item, select a number from -3 to 3, and fill that number in the ESL Table.

-3 = totally dissatisfied,

3 = totally satisfied,

0 = the neutral point (the point at which the respondent is about equally satisfied and dissatisfied).

For example, if a respondent thinks the contribution of the income factor to life satisfaction is "-3", that indicates the respondent is totally dissatisfied with his or her income. The income factor brings him or her lots of *pain*. If a respondent thinks the contribution of the income factor to life satisfaction is "3", that indicates the respondent is totally satisfied with his or her income. The income factor brings him or her lots of *pleasure*.

Table 6.2 Evaluation of Satisfaction Level

The level of Satisfaction with the current life	-3	-2	-1	0	1	2	3
X_1: Health							
X_2: Job or income							
X_3: Love or marriage							
X_4: Education							
X_5: Housing and environment							
X_6: Social safety							
X_7: Transportation system							
X_8: Kinship or family							
X_9: Social status							
X_{10}: Basic rights							
X_{11}: Others							
X_{12}:							

2. **The level of happiness** H is defined as the aggregation of the emotional experiences of *pleasure* during a longer period of time. An example is the aggregation of the emotional experiences of *pleasure* during the past year.

$$H = \sum_{i=1} b_i Y_i \qquad (6.3)$$

where Y_i is a significant factor influencing *the level of happiness*, b_i is the weight of this factor (estimated by the actual amount of time spent on paying attention to the factor). b_i also stands for the degree to which individuals care about this factor, reflecting individuals' preference, where

$$\sum_{i=1} b_i = 100\%$$

The time period can be the past year, for example.

Researchers should conduct surveys in two steps. First, respondents can be asked to estimate the weights of various factors influencing *the level of happiness* during a past period of time such as the past year from memory (see Table of Weights of Happiness Factors). Second, respondents can be asked to evaluate the contribution of each factor to *the level of happiness* during a past period of time respectively (see Table of Evaluation of Happiness Level).

(1)Table of Weights of Happiness Factors (WHF)

The WHF Table shows the weights of various factors influencing *the level of happiness* during a past period of time. Researchers can ask respondents to rank the order of various factors according to the actual amount of time spent on paying attention to each factor, excluding the amount of time for sleep. For each item, select a number from 0 to 10, and fill that number in the WHF Table. B_i in the WHF Table is the number of ordering. The numbers for different factors can be the same. For example, in the past year, if a respondent focused his or her attention on the factor of work the most amount of time and focused his or her attention on the factor of education the least amount of time, then select B_2 to equal 10 and B_4 to equal 1. If the respondent paid no attention to the factor of basic rights, then select B_{10} to equal 0.

10 = the most time

1 = the least time

0 = no time

The weight b_i corresponding to the i-th factor can be transformed via B_i.

$$b_i = B_i / \sum_{i=1} B_i \qquad (6.4)$$

Table 6.3 Weights of Happiness Factors

Weights (select numbers according to the actual amount of time spent on paying attention to each factor)	10	9	8	7	6	5	4	3	2	1	0
B_1: Health											
B_2: Job or income											
B_3: Love or marriage											
B_4: Education											
B_5: Housing and Environment											
B_6: Social safety											
B_7: Transportation System											
B_8: Kinship or family											
B_9: Social status											
B_{10}: Basic rights											
B_{11}: Others											
B_{12}:											

Instructions:

B_1: Health (including the condition of receiving medical treatment)

B_2: Job or income (including investments, pensions, unemployment benefits, etc.)

B_3: Love or marriage (whether there is a lack of love or a lack of affection with partner)

B_4: Education (including their own and their children's educational conditions)

B_5: Housing and environment (including air quality, environment health, public facilities and services such as libraries, parks, and fitness centers)

B_6: Social safety (including personal and property safety, food and medicine safety, public security, etc.)

B_7: Transportation system (including commuting and traveling outside of the place of residence)

B_8: Kinship or family (including the living conditions of children, parents, brothers and sisters)

B_9: Social status (the relative position in the *Similar Reference Group*, including interpersonal relationships)

B_{10}: Basic rights (including freedom, democracy, equality, fairness, justice, respect from others, faith, and the quality of governmental services)

B_{11} and B_{12}: Other factors (ask respondents to specify what other factors that also influence their *happiness*. Examples can be natural disasters such as earthquakes and typhoons or anything else not previously covered)

(2)Table of Evaluation of Happiness Level (EHL)

The EHL Table shows respondent's evaluations of *the level of happiness* during a period of time. Respondents can be asked to evaluate the contribution of each factor to their level of *happiness* during a past period of time respectively. For each item, select a number from -3 to 3, and fill the number in the EHL Table.

-3 = the worst,

3 = the best,

0 = the neutral point (neither good nor bad).

Table 6.4 Evaluation of Happiness Level

The level of happiness	-3	-2	-1	0	1	2	3
Y_1: Health							
Y_2: Job or income							
Y_3: Love or marriage							
Y_4: Education							
Y_5: Housing and environment							
Y_6: Social safety							
Y_7: Transportation system							
Y_8: Kinship or family							
Y_9: Social status							
Y_{10}: Basic rights							
Y_{11}: Others							
Y_{12}:							

When researchers conduct surveys on groups with different characteristics, factors can be added to or deleted from the tables, and the grades of weights can be expanded or reduced. For example, if a group of respondents are secondary school students, "Job or income" should be deleted. For groups of respondents in areas prone to natural disasters, factors like earthquakes or typhoons should be added into the tables.

The index of *satisfaction level s* at a moment in time is defined below.

$$s = S \times 100 = (\sum_{i=1} a_i X_i) \times 100 \qquad (6.5)$$

The index of **happiness level h** during a period of time is defined below.

$$h = H \times 100 = (\sum_{i=1} b_i Y_i) \times 100 \qquad (6.6)$$

Because the survey itself is an approximate method to assess happiness, the absolute values of data from surveys are not important. The significance of the indexes lies in the relative results from the comparisons between individuals. The purpose of multiplying 100 is to convert the index to an integer from a decimal.

The **Well-Being Index** defined in this book consists of the index of *satisfaction level s* at a moment in time and the index of *happiness level h* during a period of time.

3.   Respondent's personal information.

Let respondents select numbers in the following questions according to their own situations.

Gender:
    ① Male
    ② Female
Health:
    ① Very healthy
    ② Occasionally has minor illnesses
    ③ Often has minor illnesses
    ④ Suffers non-serious chronic diseases
    ⑤ Suffers from serious chronic diseases
Age:
    ① 18-25
    ② 26-32

③ 33-45

④ 46-60

⑤ Over 61

Yearly income:

  ① 0

  ② Under 8,000 USD

  ③ 8,001-20,000 USD

  ④ 20,001-40,000 USD

  ⑤ 40,001-80,000 USD

  ⑥ 80,001 USD or higher

Education:

  ① Junior high school or under

  ② Senior high school or equivalent

  ③ Two or three-year college

  ④ Bachelor degree

  ⑤ Master degree

  ⑥ Ph.D.

Marital status:

  ① Married, relationship with spouse:

    (1) Very good

    (2) Good

    (3) Neither good nor bad (Neutral)

    (4) Poor

    (5) Very poor

  ② Single:

    (1) Grief from recent breakup or loss of love

    (2) Not dating

    (3) Dating without commitment

    (4) Falling in love

    (5) Being in a stable partnership

Children:
    ① None
    ② Yes:
        (1) In preschool
        (2) In elementary school
        (3) In high school
        (4) In college or university or graduate school
        (5) Employed

Job:
    ① Yes:
        (1) Very satisfied
        (2) Satisfied
        (3) Neither satisfied nor dissatisfied
        (4) Dissatisfied
        (5) Very dissatisfied
    ② None:
        (1) Unemployed
        (2) Retired
        (3) Full-time student

Housing:
    ① Own
    ② Rent

Car:
    ① Own
    ② None

Religious belief:
    ① None
    ② Yes:
        (1) Christianity
        (2) Catholic

(3) Buddhism

(4) Islam

(5) Others

By comparing a respondent's personal information with the numbers he or she filled in the tables, researchers can evaluate whether the numbers are authentic and reliable, whether the numbers truly reflect the respondent's subjective experiences, and whether the numbers can be regarded as valid, based on whether his or her answers are consistent with scientific knowledge or common sense and so forth.

The usage of the *Weighted Scales* in the survey can be illustrated with the results from the following three respondents.

(a) Respondent *A* evaluated her overall satisfaction with the current life at the moment of completing the scale. The numbers filled in Table 6.5 and Table 6.6 are as follows:

Table 6.5 Weights of Satisfaction Factors

Weights (select numbers according to the degrees of influence)	10	9	8	7	6	5	4	3	2	1	0	%
A_1: Health									2			3.9
A_2: Job or income	10											20
A_3:Love or marriage	10											20
A_4: Education										1		2
A_5: Housing and environment					6							12
A_6: Social safety						5						9.8
A_7: Transportation system						5						9.8
A_8:Kinship or family	10											20
A_9: Social status										1		2
A_{10} : Basic rights										1		2
A_{11}: Others												0
A_{12}:												0

Table 6.6 Evaluation of Satisfaction Level

The level of Satisfaction with the current life	-3	-2	-1	0	1	2	3
X_1: Health						2	
X_2: Job or income		-2					
X_3: Love or marriage				0			
X_4: Education				0			
X_5: Housing and environment			-1				
X_6: Social safety					1		
X_7: Transportation system					1		
X_8: Kinship or family						2	
X_9: Social status					1		
X_{10}: Basic rights				0			
X_{11}: Others							
X_{12}:							

Respondent *A* estimated *the level of happiness* during the past year from memory. The time period was the past year from July 1, 2010 to June 30, 2011. The numbers filled in Table 6.7 and Table 6.8 are as follows:

Table 6.7 Weights of Happiness Factors

Weights（select numbers according to the actual amount of time spent on paying attention to each factor）	10	9	8	7	6	5	4	3	2	1	0	%
B_1:　Health									2			4.4
B_2: Job or income	10											22
B_3:　Love or marriage		9										20
B_4:　Education										1		2.2
B_5: Housing and environment					6							13
B_6: Social safety							4					8.9
B_7: Transportation system						5						11
B_8: Kinship or family						5						11
B_9: Social status									2			4.4
B_{10} : Basic rights										1		2.2
B_{11}: Others												0
B_{12}:												0

Table 6.8 Evaluation of Happiness Level

The level of happiness	-3	-2	-1	0	1	2	3
Y_1: Health						2	
Y_2: Job or income		-2					
Y_3: Love or marriage				0			
Y_4: Education				0			
Y_5: Housing and environment			-1				
Y_6: Social safety				0			
Y_7: Transportation system					1		
Y_8: Kinship or family						2	
Y_9: Social status				0			
Y_{10}: Basic rights				0			
Y_{11}: Others							
Y_{12}:							

Respondent A's personal information is as follows:

Gender: Female

Health: Occasionally has minor illnesses.

Age: 18-25

Yearly Income: Under 8,000 USD

Education: Bachelor

Children: None

Marital status: Single, not dating

Job: Yes. Dissatisfied

Housing: Rent

Car: None

Religion: None

According to equations (6.2) and (6.4), Weights of Satisfaction Factors a_i can be figured out by using the EXCEL tool and are listed in the far right column in Table 6.5, Weights of Happiness Factors b_i are listed in the far right column in Table 6.7. According to equations (6.5) and (6.6), the index of *satisfaction level s* with the current life for Respondent *A* was calculated as: *s* = 18. The index of *happiness level h* during the past year for Respondent *A* was calculated as: *h* = -16

Assume that Respondent *A* honestly answered to the scales, the answers truly reflected her subjective experiences, the following conclusions can be drawn from her answers. The main factor influencing *the level of satisfaction* with the current life was the factor of "Job or income". The positive value of the index of *satisfaction level* shows that Respondent *A* was more satisfied than dissatisfied with her current life. In the past year, the main factor influencing the level of *happiness* was also the factor of "Job or income". The minus value of the index of *happiness level* shows that the amount of *pain* was greater than that of *pleasure* during the past year. The employment issues are related to both individuals and governments, individuals need to improve their skills and abilities, while governments need to create more opportunities of employment. Respondent *A* can be assumed to be a recently graduated college student without working for a long time according to her personal information. Her dissatisfaction with work is consistent with common situations. The survey results can be considered valid.

(b)Respondent *B* evaluated his overall satisfaction with the current life at the moment of completing the scale. The numbers filled in Table 6.9 and Table 6.10 are as follows:

Table 6.9 Weights of Satisfaction Factors

Weights	10	9	8	7	6	5	4	3	2	1	0	%
A_1: Health				7								13
A_2: Job or income	10											18
A_3: Love or marriage					6							11
A_4: Education					6					1		11
A_5: Housing and environment			7									13
A_6: Social safety						5						9.1
A_7: Transportation system							4					7.3
A_8: Kinship or family					6							11
A_9: Social status										1		1.8
A_{10}: Basic rights									2			3.6
A_{11}: Typhoon										1		1.8
A_{12}:												0

Table 6.10 Evaluation of Satisfaction Level

The level of Satisfaction with the current life	-3	-2	-1	0	1	2	3
X_1: Health						2	
X_2: Job or income					1		
X_3: Love or marriage						2	
X_4: Education					1		
X_5: Housing and environment				0			
X_6: Social safety	-3						
X_7: Transportation system			-1				
X_8: Kinship or family						2	
X_9: Social status				0			
X_{10}: Basic rights		-2					
X_{11}: Typhoon		-2					
X_{12}:							

Respondent *B* estimated *the level of happiness* during the past year from memory. The time period was the past year from August 20, 2010 to August 19, 2011. The numbers filled in Table 6.11 and Table 6.12 are as follows:

Table 6.11 Weights of Happiness Factors

Weights	10	9	8	7	6	5	4	3	2	1	0	%
B_1: Health									3			9.7
B_2: Job or income	10											32
B_3: Love or marriage							4					13
B_4: Education			8									26
B_5: Housing and environment											0	0
B_6: Social safety										1		3.2
B_7: Transportation system										1		3.2
B_8: Kinship or family							4					13
B_9: Social status											0	0
B_{10}: Basic rights											0	0
B_{11}: Others												0
B_{12}:												0

Table 6.12 Evaluation of Happiness Level

The level of happiness	-3	-2	-1	0	1	2	3
Y_1: Health						2	
Y_2: Job or income					1		
Y_3: Love or marriage					1		
Y_4: Education				0			
Y_5: Housing and environment				0			
Y_6: Social safety		-2					
Y_7: Transportation system			-1				
Y_8: Kinship or family						2	
Y_9: Social status				0			
Y_{10}: Basic rights			-1				
Y_{11}: Others							
Y_{12}:							

Respondent B's personal information is as follows:

Gender: Male

Health: Very healthy

Age: 33-45

Yearly Income: 40,001-80,000 USD

Education: Master

Children: In preschool and elementary school

Marital status: Married, and having a good relationship with his wife.

Job: Yes. Neither satisfied nor dissatisfied

Housing: Own

Car: Own

Religion: None

According to equations (6.2) and (6.4), Weights of Satisfaction Factors a_i can be figured out and are listed in the far right column in Table 6.9, Weights of Happiness Factors b_i are listed in the far right column in Table 6.11. According to equations (6.5) and (6.6), the index of *satisfaction level s* with the current life for Respondent B was calculated as: $s = 53$. The index of *happiness level h* during the past year for Respondent B was calculated as: $h = 81$.

Assume that Respondent B honestly answered to the scales, the answers truly reflected his subjective experiences, the following conclusions can be drawn from his answers. The main factor influencing *the level of satisfaction* with the current life was the factor of "Job or income". Respondent B is most dissatisfied with the factor of "Social safety". In the past year, the main factor influencing the level of *happiness* was also the factor of "Job or income". "Social safety" was the main factor leading to negative influences on the respondent's *happiness* level. The "Social safety" factors can be solved only by the government. These issues cannot be solved by individuals. Respondent B's personal information and his answers showed no obvious contradiction to common sense. The survey results can be considered valid.

(c)Respondent C evaluated his overall satisfaction with the current life at the moment of completing the scale. The numbers filled in Table 6.13 and Table 6.14 are as follows:

Table 6.13 Weights of Satisfaction Factors

Weights	10	9	8	7	6	5	4	3	2	1	0	%
A_1: Health	10											21
A_2: Job or income						5						11
A_3: Love or marriage					6							13
A_4: Education										1		2.1
A_5: Housing and environment						5						11
A_6: Social safety					6							13
A_7: Transportation system							4					8.5
A_8: Kinship or family					6							13
A_9: Social status									2			4.3
A_{10} : Basic rights									2			4.3
A_{11}: Others												0
A_{12}:												0

Table 6.14 Evaluation of Satisfaction Level

The level of Satisfaction with the current life	-3	-2	-1	0	1	2	3
X_1: Health	-3						
X_2: Job or income						2	
X_3: Love or marriage					1		
X_4: Education				0			
X_5: Housing and environment					2		
X_6: Social safety			-1				
X_7: Transportation system			-1				
X_8: Kinship or family					1		
X_9: Social status				0			
X_{10}: Basic rights				0			
X_{11}: Others							
X_{12}:							

Respondent C estimated *the level of happiness* during the past year from memory. The time period was the past year from June 1, 2010 to May 31, 2011. The numbers filled in Table 6.15 and Table 6.16 are as follows:

Table 6.15 Weights of Happiness Factors

Weights	10	9	8	7	6	5	4	3	2	1	0	%
B_1: Health	10											30
B_2: Job or income								3				9.1
B_3: Love or marriage							4					12
B_4: Education										1		3
B_5: Housing and environment									2			6.1
B_6: Social safety							4					12
B_7: Transportation system								3				9.1
B_8: Kinship or family								3				9.1
B_9: Social status									2			6.1
B_{10}: Basic rights										1		3
B_{11}: Others												0
B_{12}:												0

Table 6.16 Evaluation of Happiness Level

The level of happiness	-3	-2	-1	0	1	2	3
Y_1: Health	-3						
Y_2: Job or income						2	
Y_3: Love or marriage					1		
Y_4: Education				0			
Y_5: Housing and environment						2	
Y_6: Social safety			-1				
Y_7: Transportation system			-1				
Y_8: Kinship or family					1		
Y_9: Social status					1		
Y_{10}: Basic rights					1		
Y_{11}: Others							
Y_{12}:							

Respondent C's personal information is as follows:

Gender: Male

Health: Suffers from serious chronic diseases.

Age: Over 61

Yearly Income: 20,001-40,000 USD

Education: Bachelor

Children: Employed

Marital status: Married, and having a good relationship with his wife.

Job: None, retired

Housing: Own

Car: Own

Religion: None

According to equations (6.2) and (6.4), Weights of Satisfaction Factors a_i are listed in the far right column in Table 6.13, Weights of Happiness Factors b_i are listed in the far right column in Table 6.15. According to equations (6.5) and (6.6), the index of *satisfaction level* s with the current life for Respondent C was calculated as: $s = -17$. The index of *happiness level* h during the past year for Respondent C was calculated as: $h = -52$

Assume that Respondent C honestly answered to the scales, the answers truly reflected his subjective experiences, the following conclusions can be drawn from his answers. The main factor influencing Respondent C's level of satisfaction with the current life was the factor of health. The most important problem of Respondent C was suffering from serious chronic diseases. In the past year, the main factor influencing his level of *happiness* was also the factor of health. General speaking, the problem of suffering from diseases comes mainly from personal factors. The government has no direct responsibility. Respondent C can be assumed to be a retiree from his personal information. It is common sense that an elderly person is likely to suffer from serious chronic diseases. The survey results can be considered valid.

As can be seen from the three examples above, for some people, the main factors influencing their level of *happiness* come from personal factors; for some others, the main factors influencing their level of *happiness* come from governmental policies and so forth; for some other people, the main factors influencing their level of *happiness* come from both personal and governmental factors.

Chapter 7

Explanations of Certain Social Phenomena

Basic Hypotheses and Views

There are five basic hypotheses and views in this book.

1. The Dual Nature of Human Selfishness and Altruism

Dawkins argued in his book entitled *The Selfish Gene* that, "a predominant quality to be expected in a successful gene is ruthless selfishness. This gene selfishness will usually give rise to selfishness in individual behaviour" (Dawkins, 2006, p.2). "We are born selfish" (Dawkins, 2006, p.3).

His point of view is reasonable to some extent. However, this book does not fully agree with this viewpoint, and argues that a gene is selfish from the perspective of competition between genes. But when a gene and its offspring are in conflict, this gene will behave unselfishly. It will sacrifice itself and give the chance of survival to its offspring. Only in this way, is it most beneficial for the gene to reproduce from generation to generation. When a gene and its offspring are in conflict, if this gene is still absolutely selfish, its offspring will die, and eventually, it will die too. As a result, the kind of absolutely selfish gene must have been eliminated long ago in the evolutionary process. Thus, the gene has the dual nature of selfishness and altruism. It can be inferred from the above analyses that, when an individual's interests conflict with the interests of his or her offspring, the offspring's interests take precedence. For example, when a pregnant mother lacks calcium and starts taking calcium supplements, the calcium is first used to meet the needs of the unborn fetus, while the remainder is used by the mother. Sometimes, when an expectant mother takes large doses of calcium supplements during pregnancy, she may still lack calcium since fetal demands are high. But after birth, if the mother still takes calcium, she will soon have enough of it for her own needs.

Since humans are social animals, when individuals live in a group, there is competition, as well as cooperation and interdependence. In a group, an absolutely selfish individual will eventually be cast out by the group. As a result, individuals' selfishness is limited under constraints of social ethics, law, culture, etc. Individuals must have a certain degree of altruism, so as to reach equilibriums between individuals and their group as well as between individuals and their environments.

The reason for this is that "a group, such as a species or a population within a species, whose individual members are prepared to sacrifice themselves for the welfare of the group, may be less likely to go extinct than a rival group whose individual members place their own selfish interests first. Therefore, the world becomes populated mainly by groups consisting of self-sacrificing individuals. This is the theory of 'group selection' , long assumed to be true by biologists not familiar with the details of evolutionary theory, brought out into the open in a famous book by V. C. Wynne-Edwards" (Dawkins, 2006, p.7)

This indicates that individuals existing in the world have a certain degree of altruism and spirit of self-sacrifice. Nations or races composed of absolutely selfish individuals were eliminated long ago in the competition for survival.

Individuals with the dual nature of selfishness and altruism, behave differently at different times, under different environments. Whether individuals behave selfishly or altruistically depends on the environments in which they live and on whom they encounter. Individuals behave more altruistically when survival of their group is endangered. Individuals behave more selfishly when there is no threat to the survival of their group. In times of peace, in order to survive, individuals encountering other competitors behave more selfishly in work and in life. But, "the commonest and most conspicuous acts of animal altruism are done by parents, especially mothers, towards their children" (Dawkins, 2006, p.6). For humans, altruism is also exhibited in parental love towards their children. Such altruism is beneficial to the survival and continuity of future generations.

Human altruism is derived or sublimated from the altruism towards offspring. Human altruism is also exhibited in the situation when a group is endangered, whose individual members may sacrifice their own lives for the long-term benefit of their group. When a nation faced extinction, many heroic individuals would sacrifice themselves for the good of their motherland as, should their country face disaster, their descendants would not survive or would lead terrible lives. These groups have a stronger ability to survive, compared to groups consisting of absolutely selfish individuals. Throughout history, numerous national heroes and martyrs sacrificed their own lives for their motherlands to ensure their security and provide a good environment for their descendants. "In wartime, people make great personal sacrifices for the good of their group. As Winston Churchill said of the Battle of Britain, the actions of the Royal Air Force pilots were genuinely altruistic: A great many people owed a great deal to those who flew into battle knowing there was a high probability—70 percent for those on a standard tour of duty— they would not return" (Myers, 2005, p.528).

2. Survival and Reproduction Being Primary

"It is important to realize that seeking pleasure is a reflex response built into our genes for the preservation of the species, not for the purpose of our own personal advantage. The pleasure we take in eating is an efficient way to ensure that the body will get the nourishment it needs. The pleasure of sexual intercourse is an equally practical method for the genes to program the body to reproduce and thereby to ensure the continuity of the genes" (Csikszentmihalyi, 1990, p.17). In other words, *pleasure* is a way to benefit individuals' survival and reproduction. Therefore survival and reproduction are primary, *pleasure* and *happiness* are secondary.

The consequences of long-term evolution are that the majority of features associated with *pleasure* and *happiness* are beneficial to individuals' survival and reproduction. In a long process of evolution, all features that are beneficial to survival and reproduction were preserved and strengthened. Those who possess these features have a stronger ability to adapt to differing environments, and their descendants were then able to survive and reproduce. Those who do not possess these features have a weaker ability to adapt to differing environments, and their descendants were eliminated after a long process of evolution. Because our ancestors had many features that were beneficial to survival and reproduction, we are alive today. These features are preserved in our genes and in our human nature.

Individuals do not pursue *pleasure* every moment. Individuals often do painful things to survive. For example, some people hate their jobs, but to survive, they go to work everyday. Individuals currently living in the world are those who are the most beneficial to survival and reproduction, not the most beneficial to the enjoyment of *pleasure* and *happiness*.

3. Rational Individuals Pursuing Long-term Happiness

An external stimulus that produces *pleasure* is not necessarily beneficial to survival and reproduction. This is just like that a tiger has four legs, but an animal with four legs is not necessarily a tiger. For instance, drugs change the *brain physiological state* directly and produce an intensive experience of *pleasure* for a short period of time. But if being taken for a long period of time, drugs can cause considerable harm to one's survival and reproduction. In the same way, an external stimulus that produces negative feelings is not necessarily harmful to survival and reproduction. For instance, a bitter pill can be healthy even though it tastes bad.

At the physiological level, responses in the brain follow scientific laws. Human's sense organs cannot usually distinguish whether or not there is a toxin in delicious food. The physiological reward is embodied in the sense organs and the brain can sense that the food is tasty. The psychological reward is related to hereditary and environmental factors, as well as states of consciousness. It needs cognitive evaluations.

If an individual merely pursues short-term *pleasure,* it can sometimes bring long-term harm to him or her. A rational individual should pursue and deal with matters that are beneficial to survival and reproduction. In this process, the individual can naturally experience *pleasure.* Accordingly, he or she can achieve long-term *happiness* more easily.

Rational individuals pursue maximum *happiness* for the long term or for their entire life or eternity, instead of pursuing transient *pleasure* for the short term. Rational individuals can sacrifice their current benefits for the long-term benefits of the future. "People are willing, at times, to sacrifice momentary positive affect for other goals that they value. For example, Kim-Prieto found that Asian and Asian American students were more likely to choose tasks that met their parents' approval or tasks that would lead to achievement over other tasks that were described as fun and personally enjoyable" (Diener, 2009b, pp.87-88).

If something yields a long-term benefit, even if it is painful in the short-term, rational individuals will do it. For greater and long-lasting *happiness*, some individuals may even sacrifice benefits of this life for the next life, such as ascetic monks who believe in reincarnation or afterlife, or some individuals who sacrifice their lives for their ideals.

4. A Hierarchy of Three Stages

In the words of Bentham, "nature has placed mankind under the governance of two sovereign masters, pain and pleasure. It is for them alone to point out what we ought to do, as well as to determine what we shall do. On the one hand the standard of right and wrong, on the other the chain of causes and effects, are fastened to their throne" (Bentham, 2006, p.1). Mill, in his book *Utilitarianism,* argued that "the ultimate end, with reference to and for the sake of which all other things are desirable (whether we are considering our own good or that of other people), is an existence exempt as far as possible from pain, and as rich as possible in enjoyments, both in point of quantity and quality" (Mill, 2003, p.190).

While borrowing the concepts of intensity and duration from Bentham's definition of happiness, this book does not fully agree with the stated utilitarian values, because priority should be placed on getting workable solutions to problems related to survival and reproduction.

In modern society, individuals' survival relies on the group in which individuals live. It is difficult for a single individual to survive alone. So when individuals' interests conflict with the group's interests, the group's interests take precedence. When individuals' survival and reproduction conflict with seeking *pleasure*, survival and reproduction take precedence.

A hierarchy of three stages of individuals' pursuits is proposed below. When one stage is substantially satisfied, the next stage becomes dominant.

The first stage is survival of the group in which individuals live. Individuals behave more altruistically when survival of their group is threatened and endangered.

The second stage is individuals' survival and reproduction. Individuals behave more selfishly when there is no threat and danger to survival of their group.

The third stage is the pursuit of *happiness*. Individuals pursue *pleasure* and avoid *pain* more often when there is no threat and danger to survival of both individuals and their group. For example, some powerful persons chase *pleasure* incessantly regardless of the consequences. Some dudes constantly look for new thrills and stimulation.

Individuals with the aforementioned characteristics are most likely to survive and reproduce their descendants. Therefore, the utilitarian principle of hedonism is conditionally valid and correct, only when there is no threat and danger to survival and reproduction of individuals and their groups.

5. Several Exceptions

Like other social studies, the conclusions and inferences in this theory are drawn from statistical data. Therefore, they are valid for the majority of people, but not necessarily applicable to every individual. For example, a few individuals having a strong will can control their attention, and more frequently focus their attention on wonderful imaginations, on good future expectations, on good results from cognitive evaluations, or are often in a deep meditative state. Thus, they can experience *pleasure* for a relatively long period of time, and achieve greater *happiness* in their lives. A few spiritual masters, saints and monks can reach such a state and level. But living in this lifestyle, they must have their basic *needs* for survival met first. It is very difficult for most ordinary people to practice to such an extent and therefore their lifestyles do not have universal significance. Their lifestyles can mentally have an important impact on *happiness*, but can not directly and completely eliminate people's *pain* from the material aspects such as hunger, illness, bad living conditions, unemployment, natural disasters, etc. These problems must be solved by science and technology, as well as economic development.

Answers to Frequently Asked Questions

Just as a theory of natural science is able to explain scientific experimental results, a theory of social science should be able to give reasonable explanations for social phenomena statistically. This integrated theory seems to answer, or partly answer the following questions.

1. Are there universals in *happiness* for most people?

Yes. This is like that everyone's heart is different, but electrocardiograms of most people are similar. Everyone's eyes are different, but the function of the eye is the same. Although individuals differ from one another, they show coherence in their behavior across time or place. Therefore, although everyone is different, there are common features in *happiness* for most people.

2. Can we measure *pleasure* scientifically?

Theoretically, we can. As stated in Chapter 5, under certain experimental conditions that only one variable changes while the other variables remain unchanged, researchers can figure out the amount of *pleasure* within a shorter period of time by means of measuring the change in the *brain physiological state* using EEG techniques and so forth.

3. Can we measure *happiness* scientifically?

Theoretically, it is possible. For example, as stated in Chapter 6, researchers could figure out the total amount of *happiness* within one year by continuously recording a respondent's *brain physiological state* for 365 days. However, it is very difficult to make it really happen with the current technology and experimental instruments.

4. Can we measure a respondent's level of life satisfaction at a given moment in time scientifically?

Theoretically, it is possible. An individual's *brain physiological states* are different in different situations when the person makes a positive evaluation or a negative evaluation of life satisfaction. However, it is very difficult to make it really happen with the current technology and experimental instruments. In addition, it is very difficult to design an experimental condition that can make the experimental results be unique for the same event.

5. How do people's values influence *happiness*?

In the process of the formation of one's values, an individual's behavior and experience leave memory traces in his or her brain, and thus influence the brain's growth and architecture. According to the *Integration* of *Pleasure Intensity*, whether an individual can experience *pleasure* at a time is related to the memory traces in the brain at that time. These memory traces influence an individual's *happiness* during longer periods of time.

6. How does personality influence *happiness*?

Hereditary factors include personality traits. The physical brain includes hereditary factors. Everyone's brain is different. According to the *Integration* of *Pleasure Intensity,* whether an individual can experience *pleasure* at a time is related to the hereditary factors of the brain at that time. These hereditary factors influence an individual's *happiness* during longer periods of time.

7. How do cultures have an effect on *happiness*?

In the process of individuals' growth, environmental factors leave memory traces in the brain. In different cultural environments, an individual's behavior and experience leave different memory traces in his or her brain. According to the *Integration* of *Pleasure Intensity,* whether an individual can experience *pleasure* at a time is related to the memory traces in the brain at that time. These memory traces influence an individual's *happiness* during longer periods of time.

8. Is health a key to *happiness*?

Good health is a necessary condition for *happiness*, but not a sufficient condition. Health is one of the *Essential Factors*. Without good health, people feel *pain*. With good health, people do not feel the *pain* from bad health, but they may not necessarily feel *happiness* for a long period of time because there are other factors influencing *happiness*.

9. Can people make themselves happier?

Yes. People can increase the frequency and duration of *pleasures* by degrading their thresholds of *pleasures*, rationally selecting their *Similar Reference Groups* and so forth. People can make their *Individual Features* match or fit into their environments by means of enhancing abilities and skills, changing values or changing their environments.

10. Why were increases in wealth associated with only small increases in *happiness* in wealthier nations?

Reasons for this include, but are not limited to, the following:

(1) Misunderstanding of *happiness*

Many of us lack a correct understanding of *happiness* and its features. We often overestimate the level of *happiness* of others. We tend to be dissatisfied when we don't have something that others have. It is natural to think that other people are enjoying *happiness* from what they have. In reality, other people's possessions may not necessarily make them happy, and they may also be experiencing *pain* from other things that they lack.

We often assume that other people are happier than us.

For instance, we only see the glossy side of movie stars, but have little insight into their troubles and enormous pressures. Negative emotional experiences are generated in the process of overcoming the difficulties and handling the pressures. Behind the scenes, their lives are not necessarily all glitz and glamorous. Consequently their level of *happiness* is generally overestimated.

We tend to believe that after achieving our goals, we can achieve long-lasting joy and *happiness*. However, *happiness* is a process of pleasant experiences during a period of time, not just an end state that results when things go well. After accomplishing a goal or realizing an ideal, the intensive experiences of *pleasure* and excitement will gradually weaken and may eventually disappear.

This erroneous understanding of *happiness* does not directly correlate to the accumulation of wealth.

(2) *Preference of Attention*

Since survival is a primary instinct, attention is more likely to be focused on events that lead to negative emotions. After the biggest problem is solved, the second biggest problem takes its place. As a nation's economy develops, material problems decrease, but the basic mental problems people often have change little. Problems associated with love, family and interpersonal relationships are almost the same before and after the economic development. Owing to the *Preference of Attention*, lots of *pleasure* factors are idle most of the time because attention is not focused on them. Therefore, their influences on *happiness* are small.

(3) *Wooden Barrel Principle*

According to the *Wooden Barrel Principle,* an individual's level of *happiness* in a lifetime depends on the height and the duration of the short planks. In addition, people are more likely to make such a mistake as "patching one hole and expanding another". For example, when people lack money, the process of earning money by working overtime could harm their health, or impact the harmony of their family by reducing time spent nurturing the relationship. In the process of the "plank" of money being lengthened, the "plank" of health or kinship is shortened.

(4) After the increase in wealth, the *Adaptation*, *Relativity*, *Regression* and *Asymmetry* of *Pleasure Intensity* are all still playing the same roles. These features of *Pleasure Intensity* do not directly correlate to the accumulation of wealth.

11. Why is the influence of money on *happiness* "*diminishing marginal utility*"?

The reasons can be given in at least the three aspects below.

(1) *Diminishing marginal response* of the *brain physiological state*

Because the response in the brain to external stimulation is *diminishing marginal response, Pleasure Intensity* originated from external stimulation is also *diminishing marginal Pleasure Intensity*. As a result, the influence of money (an external stimulus) on *happiness* is "*diminishing marginal utility*".

(2) *Preference of Attention*

Because of material shortages, people are likely to feel *pain*. Without basic necessary material conditions for *happiness*, then there is no a neutral platform for *happiness*, people are unlikely to experience *pleasure* for a long time. Because of material shortages, the *Preference of Attention* makes people more often focus their attention on the deficient materials that cause *pain*. Owing to the *Integration of Pleasure Intensity*, when a *pleasure* event occurs, the level of *pleasure* is reduced or offset by *pain* factors. Moreover, sometimes a person can have a *pleasure* event, but the duration of experiencing the *pleasure* from the event is likely to be relatively short because their attention involuntarily shifts to some *pain* factors and stays there.

In the process of going from having no money to having a little money, people first have to satisfy the basic *needs* for survival, to reduce *pain* factors, and weaken the level of *pain*. Money can directly and clearly solve the problems of material shortages that cause *pain*, and provide people with necessary material conditions for *happiness*. With a neutral platform, people can experience more *pleasure* when a *pleasure* event occurs. Therefore, in the stage from the material shortages to the basic living conditions being satisfied, the influence of money on *happiness* is direct and significant.

(3) *Wooden Barrel Principle*

When people's basic living conditions are met, the shortest plank of material aspects has been lengthened, but the planks of other factors such as love, kinship, friendship, etc., may become the new short planks. These new short planks then become the major factors influencing *happiness*. These mental short planks can not be directly lengthened with money. For example, a wealthy man can not directly buy true love, health, kinship and friend with money.

12. Why do religious people tend on average to experience greater *happiness* than nonreligious people (Diener, 2009a, p.213)?

People involved in religion may be happier than others for many reasons. The *Equivalence Principle* proposed in this book may be a major one of them.

A dedicated member of churches subjectively believes that he or she will go to Heaven and live happily with God forever in the future. While thinking of this wonderful life in the future, he or she feels *pleasure* because changes in the *brain physiological state* are happening. The event that such a person anticipates, i.e. that he or she will live in Heaven in the future, does not happen for the time being. However, when a person subjectively believes that an event will definitely happen, such an event has already influenced his or her *brain physiological state* and this has the same influence as if the anticipated event actually happened.

People's lives are filled with a lot of events. Major life events, such as changing jobs, getting married and having children, have a greater impact on their *happiness*. Minor life events, such as having a good meal or buying new clothes, have a slighter impact on their *happiness*. Many frustrating and annoying daily events may have a slight impact on the *happiness* of the dedicated churchgoers when they often think about the important event of going to Heaven in the future.

Religious people often participate in religious activities, study religious books and imagine a happy life in the future.

Pleasant moods and emotions occur easily and frequently. In other words, they have more positive emotional experiences, or they tend to judge their lives in more positive ways because they definitely believe in having a brilliant future. Therefore, such religious people generally experience greater *happiness* than nonreligious people.

Some religious individuals do not experience greater *happiness* than people who are not religious (Diener, 2009a, p.30). The reason is probably because these religious individuals may not really believe religion in their mind. They may seemingly believe religion or partly believe religion, but are not pious believers. In this case, the *Equivalence Principle* does not work. When they anticipate future, the changes in electrochemical activity leading to the experience of *pleasure* do not take place in their brains.

Chapter 8

Summary and Conclusions

Key Elements and Main Conclusions

(1) This theory stresses time-dependency of *happiness*, distinguishing between a cognitive evaluation of life satisfaction at a moment in time and a process of pleasant experiences during a period of time.

(2) *Happiness* during a past period of time is the aggregation of subjective emotional experiences during the period of time, rather than a cognitive evaluation of *happiness* during the period of time made afterwards.

(3) *Pleasure Intensity* at any time is determined by the *brain physiological state* at the time. The *brain physiological state* at any time is the result of the interaction of all external stimuli and internal physiological factors, as well as the state of consciousness at the time.

(4) The *brain physiological state* at any time determines the states of consciousness at the time. Simultaneously, states of consciousness also influence the *brain physiological state*. The mutual influence and interaction between states of consciousness and the *brain physiological state* reach a dynamic equilibrium.

(5) A perceived future event that does not happen at the present time may influence an individual's current

169

emotional experiences and cognitive evaluations according to the *Equivalence Principle*.

(6) The features of the *brain physiological state* are *Time-Dependency*, *Individuality*, *Integration*, *Threshold*, *Saturation*, *Adaptation*, *Relativity*, *Regression*, *Asymmetry*, *Attention*, and *Equivalence*.

(7) The features of *Pleasure Intensity* are *Subjectivity*, *Time-Dependency*, *Individuality*, *Integration*, *Threshold*, *Saturation*, *Adaptation*, *Relativity*, *Regression*, *Asymmetry*, *Attention*, and *Equivalence*. Except *Subjectivity*, all other features of *Pleasure Intensity* are similar and closely connected to the features of the *brain physiological state*.

(8) Human has the dual nature of selfishness and altruism. Individuals behave differently at different times, under different environments. Whether individuals behave selfishly or altruistically depends on the environments in which they live and on whom they encounter.

(9) There is a hierarchy of three stages for rational individuals' pursuits. The first stage is survival of the group in which individuals live. Individuals behave more altruistically when survival of their group is threatened and endangered. The second stage is individuals' survival and reproduction. Individuals behave more selfishly when there is no threat and danger to survival of their group. The third stage is the pursuit of *happiness*. Individuals pursue *pleasure* and avoid *pain* more often when there is no threat and danger to survival of both individuals and their group.

(10) Rational individuals pursue maximum *happiness* in their lifetimes, and more pursue long-term *happiness*, rather than short-term *pleasure*.

(11) The consequences of long-term evolution are that individuals currently living in the world are those who are the most beneficial to survival and reproduction, not the most beneficial to the enjoyment of *pleasure* and *happiness*.

(12) The level of *happiness* in an individual's entire life is determined by the importance and the duration of the factors that are deficient or harmful to the person.

(13) Happy individuals are in the neutral emotional state most of the time in their lifetime. They are often in the emotional state of *pleasure,* very rarely in the emotional state of *pain*. Unhappy individuals are in the emotional state of *pain* most of the time in their lifetime. They are sometimes in the neutral emotional state, very rarely in the emotional state of *pleasure*.

(14) There are many sources of *pleasure*. Different kinds of *pleasures* originated from different sources can not replace each other.

(15) Selective attention invalidates the superposition principle in physics. Some factors may influence *pleasure* at a time, but may not influence *pleasure* at another time.

(16) *Pleasure* during a short period of time can be measured using scientific methods.

(17) There are always some individuals in society who achieve far less *happiness* than others in their lifetime because of the *Relativity* of *Pleasure Intensity*.

(18) Individuals may achieve long-term *happiness* relatively easily when their *Individual Features* match their environments.

(19) The scales of *well-being* should contain weights of various factors influencing *happiness*. For different

individuals, the weights are different. For the same individual, the weights vary across time and situations.

(20) The conclusions and inferences in this theory are drawn from statistical data. They are valid for the majority of people, but may not necessarily be applicable to every individual.

Elements of Existing Theories of Happiness Incorporated in This Theory

There are many theories or models of happiness. This theory is an integrated theory that incorporates the major existing theories of happiness. For example, *Regression* of *Pleasure Intensity* of this theory contains elements of the "set-point" theory (Diener, 2009a, p.9) and the hedonic treadmill theory (Diener, 2009a, p.64). *Relativity* of *Pleasure Intensity* contains elements of the comparison theory (Diener, 2009a, p.45) and the range-frequency theory (Diener, 2009a, p.45). *Adaptation* contains elements of the adaptation theory (Diener, 2009a, p.45) and the hedonic treadmill theory (Diener, 2009a, p.64). *Individuality* contains elements of the personality theory (Diener, 2009a, p.78) and the temperament theory (Diener, 2009a, p.94). *Attention* contains elements of the attention theory (Diener, 2009a, p.114). *Asymmetry* contains the idea of inequitable reactions of positive feelings and negative feelings. *Integration* and *Individuality* contain elements of the top-down approach (Diener, 2009a, p.42). *Time-Dependency* and the definition of *happiness* contain elements of the bottom-up theory (Diener, 2009a, p.42). In addition, the

Wooden Bowl Model or *Integration* of *Pleasure Intensity* contains elements from the "broaden-and-build theory" (Diener, 2009a, p.63), the Human Nature theory (Diener, 2009a, p.138), the Self-Determination Theory (Diener, 2009a, p.138), the idea of person-environment fit (Diener, 2009a, p.39) and environmental factors such as values and cultures. The *Wooden Bowl Model or Integration, Attention, Threshold* contain elements from the goal theory (Diener, 2009a, p.38), the need theory (Diener, 2009a, p.38), the activity theory (Diener, 2009a, p.41), the judgment theory (Diener, 2009a, p.44), or called associationistic theories(Diener, 2009a, p.43), the evaluation theory (Diener, 2009a, p.139), the Hedonism theory, the desire theory, the objective list theory (Peterson, 2010, pp.255-256), and so forth.

Contributions or Possible Contributions Made by This Theory

This theory does not merely list the major existing theories of happiness. It may also make the following contributions to the theory of happiness.

(1) This theory presents the concept of the *brain physiological state* that constructs a bridge between the physiological quantity and the psychological magnitude of the brain.

(2) The *brain physiological state* at any moment in time is an integrated result of the interaction of all external stimuli, all internal physiological factors and states of

consciousness.

(3) This integrated result does not have the characteristics of the superposition principle in physics. The integrated result is neither the linear superposition, nor the non-linear superposition. The integrated result related to states of consciousness does not follow an unchanging law.

(4) This theory illustrates the physiological mechanism of experiencing *pleasure* with the *Wooden Bowl Model*.

(5) More than ten features of the *brain physiological state* are summarized based on some scientific experimental results.

(6) This theory stresses time-dependency of *need*, analyzes short-term *need*, long-term *need*, continuous *need* and cyclical *need*.

(7) This theory stresses time-dependency of *happiness*. *Pleasure* during a shorter period of time and *happiness* during a longer period of time are defined.

(8) This theory uses the concept of *pleasure* during a short period of time to analyze problems, constructs relationships between the *brain physiological state* and *Pleasure Intensity*, proposes *Individuality, Integration, Threshold, Saturation, Attention, Equivalence of Pleasure Intensity*. More than ten features of *Pleasure Intensity* are summarized based on the features of the *brain physiological state*.

(9) Various sources of *pleasure* are summarized and classified.

(10) The *Equivalence Principle* of the *brain physiological state* is proposed.

(11) This theory explains one cause of *happiness* from

religious belief using the *Equivalence Principle.*

(12) This theory proposes the *Preference of Attention.*

(13) With the *Wooden Barrel Principle,* this theory specifies that the level of *happiness* in a lifetime of an individual is determined by the height and the duration of the short planks

(14) Various factors influencing *happiness* are classified into three categories of *Essential Factors, Pleasure Factors* and *Essential—Pleasure Factors.*

(15) Necessary conditions for *happiness* are summarized.

(16) This theory proposes the dual nature of human selfishness and altruism.

(17) With the concept of total differential and partial derivatives, this theory illustrates that *pleasure* can be measured by means of scientific experiments, hypothesizes a quantitative measurement of *happiness* using the scientific method, proposes a direction and approach of measuring *happiness* using scientific methods.

(18) Analyses indicate that most individuals are in the *Neutral State* with neither *pleasure* nor *pain* most of the time in daily life.

(19) A hierarchy of three stages of individuals' pursuits is proposed. When one stage is substantially satisfied, the next stage becomes dominant.

(20) This theory integrates various seemingly independent theories and models of happiness together within a shorter period of time (tens of seconds) and within the limited space (human brain).

(21) *Individual Features* containing values are defined.

Individuals can achieve long-term *happiness* relatively easily when their *Individual Features* match their environments.

(22) This theory presents the *Weighted Scales* of *well-being*, defines the index of *satisfaction level **s*** at a moment in time and the index of *happiness level **h*** during a long period of time.

The ideas and basic framework of this theory are shown in figure 8.1.

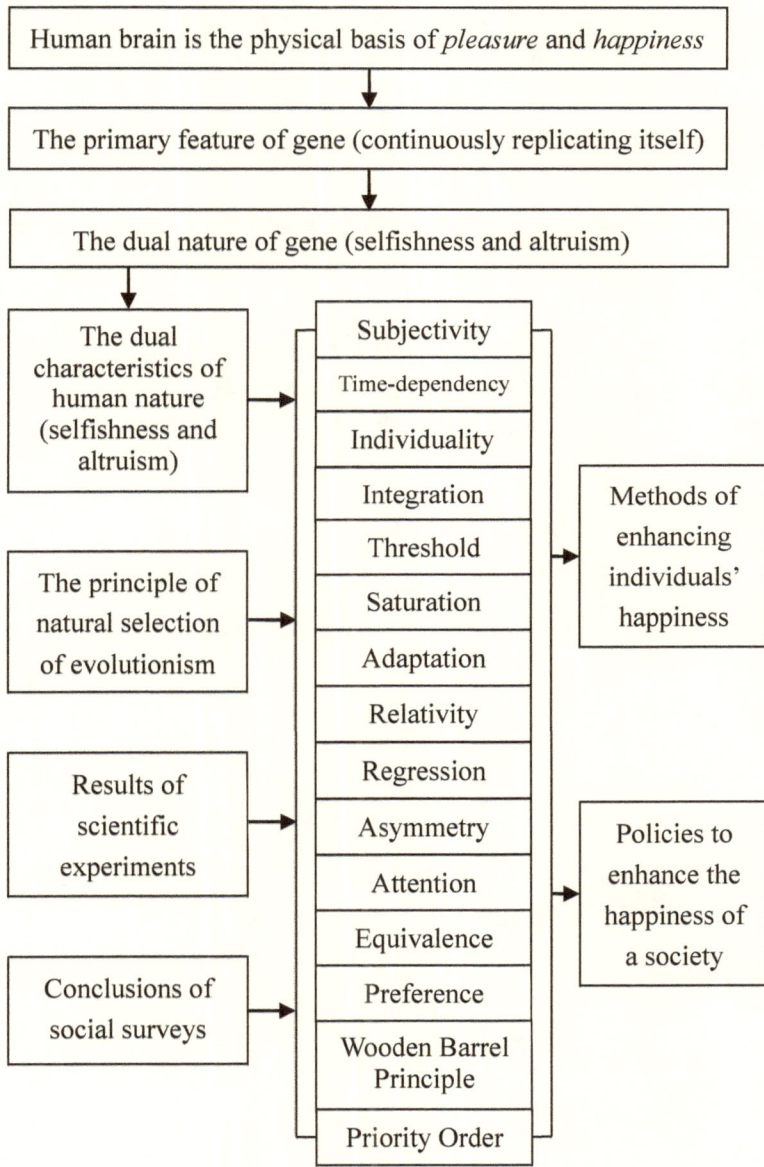

Figure 8.1

Individuals should make their *Individual Features* match or fit into their environments by means of enhancing abilities and skills, changing values or changing the environments in which they live.

Governments should improve policies and laws, etc. to build a society in which most people can easily make their *Individual Features* match or fit into their environments.

Methods of enhancing an individual's *happiness* and suggestions for enhancing the *happiness* of a society as a whole will be discussed in another book.

References

Alexander, C.K. & Sadiku, M.N.O. (2000). *Fundamentals of Electric Circuits*. Boston: The McGraw-Hill Companies, Inc.

Bentham, J. (2006). *An Introduction to the Principles of Morals and Legislation.* Xian: Shaanxi People's Publishing House

Carlson, N.R. (2005). *Foundations of physiological psychology (6th Edition)*. Boston, MA: Pearson Education, Inc.

Carr, A.(2005). *Positive Psychology: The Science of Happiness and Human Strengths*.New York, NY: Brunner-Routledge.

Cheng, T.P. (2005). *Relativity, Gravitation and Cosmology*. New York, NY: Oxford University Press.

Corbetta, M., Miezin, F.M., Dobmeyer, S., at al. (1991). Selective and Divided Attention during Visual Discriminations of Shape, Color, and Speed: Functional Anatomy by Positron Emission Tomography, *The Journal of Neuroscience, 11(8), pp.2383-2402*

Csikszentmihalyi, M. (1997). *Finding Flow: The Psychology of Engagement with Everyday Life*. New York, NY: BasicBooks, A Division of HarperCollins Publishers, Inc.

Csikszentmihalyi, M.(1990). *Flow: the Psychology of Optimal Experience*. New York, NY: Harper & Row,

Publishers, Inc.

Dawkins, R. (2006). *The Selfish Gene (30th anniversary edition)*. New York: Oxford University Press Inc.

Diener, E. (2009a). *The Science of Well-Being: The Collected Works of Ed Diener*, Social Indicators Research Series 37

Diener, E. (2009b). *Assessing Well-Being: The Collected Works of Ed Diener*, Social Indicators Research Series 39

Foot, C.J. (2009). *Atomic Physics*. Beijing: Science Press.

Ganong, W.F. (1995). *Review of Medical Physiology (17th edition)*, Norwalk, Connecticut: Appleton & Lange

Gleitman, H. (1987). *Basic Psychology (2nd Edition)*. New York, NY: W.W.Norton & Company, Inc.

Grosso, G. & Parravicini, G. P. (2006). *Solid State Physics*. Beijing: Beijing World Publishing Corporation.

Heilbroner, R.L. & Galbraith, J. K. (1987). *The Economic Problem (Revised 8th Edition)*. Englewood Cliffs, NJ: Prentice-Hall, Inc.

Hugdahl, K. (1995), *Psychophysiology: The Mind-Body Perspective*, Cambridge, MA: Harvard University Press

Hughes, M.(2002). *Sociology: the core (7th edition)*. New York, NY: The McGraw-Hill Companies, Inc.

Kaplan, W. (2004). *Advanced Calculus (5th Edition)*. Beijing: Publishing House of Electronics Industry

Klein, S. (2006). *The Science of Happiness*, New York: Marlowe & Company, An Imprint of Avalon Publishing Group, Inc.

LI, Yi-Ning, (1994). *The Share System and Modern Market Economy*. Nanjing: Jiangsu People's Press. (in Chinese)

Luck, S. J. (2005). *An Introduction to the Event-Related Potential Technique*. Cambridge, MA: The MIT Press

Lykken, D. T. (1999). *Happiness: What Studies on Twins Show Us About Nature, Nurture, and the Happiness Set Point*. New York, NY: Golden Books Publishing Co., Inc.

Mill, J. S., (2003), *Utilitarianism*, Malden, MA: Blackwell Publishing Ltd.

Myers, D. G. (2004). *Psychology (7th edition)*. New York, NY: Worth Publishers

Myers, D. G. (2005). *Social Psychology (8th edition)*. New York, NY: The McGraw-Hill Companies, Inc.

Peterson, C. (2010). *A Primer in Positive Psychology*. Beijing: China Machine Press

Richard, C. D. & James, A. S.(2001). *Introduction to electric circuits (5th edition)*. New York, NY: John Wiley & Sons, Inc

Robbins, S.P. & DeCenzo, D.A. (2007). *Fundamentals of Management (5th Edition)*. Beijing: China Renmin University Press

Seligman, M. E. P. & Royzman, E. (2003). Happiness: The Three Traditional Theories. Retrieved from http://www.authentichappiness.sas.upenn.edu/newsletter.aspx?id=49

Solso, R.L., MacLin, M. K., & MacLin, O. H. (2005). *Cognitive Psychology (7th edition)*. Boston, MA: Pearson Education, Inc.

Squire, L.R., et al, (2009). *Behavioral and cognitive neuroscience*. Beijing: Science Press.

TANG, Xiao-Wei, (2000).Laws of Brain Activation, *Chinese*

Journal of Applied Psychology, Vol. 6, No.1, p.15 (in Chinese)

Urbach, T.P., & Kutas, M.(2006). Interpreting event-related brain potential (ERP) distributions: implications of baseline potentials and variability with application to amplitude normalization by vector scaling. *Biological Psychology,* Vol.72, No.3, p.333

Index

Qiguang LI received his BSc in nuclear physics from Fudan University, his MSc and PhD in semiconductor physics from Shanghai Institute of Technical Physics of the Chinese Academy of Sciences, and his MBA from Peking University.

www.ingramcontent.com/pod-product-compliance
Lightning Source LLC
Chambersburg PA
CBHW050443290526
45786CB00006B/2138